The History of

ART TATUM,

1909 - 1932

The History of

ART TATUM,

1909 - 1932

Dr. Imelda Guyton Hunt Ph.D

Senior Publisher
Steven Lawrence Hill Sr

A Publisher Trademark Title page

ASA Publishing Corporation
An Accredited Hybrid Publishing House with the BBB
www.asapublishingcorporation.com

The Landmark Building
23 E. Front St., Suite 103, Monroe, Michigan 48161

Copyrights©2018 Dr. Imelda Guyton Hunt Ph.D, All Rights Reserved
Book Title: The History of ART TATUM, 1909 - 1932
Date Published: 06.27.2018 / Edition 1 *Trade Paperback*
Book ID: ASAPCID2380748
ISBN: 978-1-946746-29-0
Library of Congress Cataloging-in-Publication Data

This book was published in the United States of America.
Great State of Michigan

A Publisher Trademark Copyrights page

Dedicated to the memory

of

"Art Tatum and his family"

PREFACE

This is the documentation of the oral sources surrounding the life and times of Art Tatum from 1909 until 1932, including various informational interviews about his childhood, his school life, his family, his church life, his girlfriend, friends, and musical associates in Toledo, Ohio.

Other information within this autobiographical research and in the interviews conducted for this study includes who were his parents, where did they come from, when, and how did they influence his life and his music? Did Tatum play at church, and what kinds of music were played at home? What was the family's source of his musicianship? Many oral sources collected in this volume are from people who had firsthand contact with Tatum, but some are relating stories told to them by their parents or other sources, like Rose Newton, friend of Tatum's sister.

The value of all of this research is to have in one place a compiled documentation of what Tatum's life was like in Toledo, Ohio, where he lived from birth in 1909 until leaving permanently in 1932 for New York, where he was recognized in the musical world for his genius on the piano.

ACKNOWLEDGMENT

I wish to acknowledge those people who have supported me in the writing of this work. They include my daughters Nikki N. Hunt, and Gisella B. Oliver, and my grandchildren Ashlie N. Carpenter and Michael A. Carpenter, as well as Mr. and Mrs. Earskin Guyton, Rose Cannon, Toledo Public Library, Pauline Kynard, Rev. Julius Minor, Bishop Patricia McKinstry, Pierre D. Taylor, Alma L. Guyton, Thomas Vines and Carolyn Parker.

I would also like to thank the people who consented to be interviewed and who do not appear in this work—Margaret "Rusty" Monroe, Eddie Abrams, Art Edgerton, Roger Ray, John Cleveland, John Meyers, Lois Nelson, and John Mast.

Table of Contents

Preface i

Acknowledgments iii

Chapter One

Introduction 1

Methodology 6

Informant Pool 10

Written Resources Drawn Upon... 11

Oral Resources Drawn Upon 12

Review of the Literature on Art Tatum........................... 12

Historical Perspective of Toledo, Ohio 17

The Tatum Legend in Toledo 17

Art Tatum's Toledo 20

Employment and Housing in Toledo, 1909-1932 23

Toledo's Popular Culture in the Twenties 33

Prohibition, Crime, and the Licavoli Days 46

Summary 52

Chapter Two

Art Tatum, His Family and Neighbors.............................. 57

Introduction 57

Growing Up in the Tatum Family 58

Tatum's Early Problems with Vision 58

Family Life 63

Art Tatum's Relationship with His Siblings 70

A Discussion of Carl Tatum 70

Interview of Arlene Tatum Taylor 77

Related Interviews About Tatum's Family 97

Introduction 97

Interview of Casey Jones 98

Interview of Rose Newton 102

Interview of Harold Payne 108

Interview of Mozart Perry 112

Images of Tatum 115

Chapter Three

The Public Tatum, 1909-1932 119

Review of Art Tatum's Community in Toledo, Ohio 1909-1932 122

Oral Taped Interviews 128

Interview of Casey Jones 128

Interview of Gladys Herron and Jim Butler 138

Interview of Mary Belle Shealy 151

Interview of Harold Payne 163

Images of Tatum 165

Chapter Four

Tatum and other Toledo Musicians 171

Toledo's Musical Community 176

Interview of Harold Payne 190

Edited Oral Taped Interview 191

Interview of Mozart Perry and Clifford Murphy 212

Edited Taped Interview 215

Conclusions 225

Chapter Five

Conclusions 227

Influences of His Family 228

Influences of Community and Friends 234

Influences of Toledo's Musical Community... 242

References & Resources... 251

The History of

ART TATUM,

1909 - 1932

Dr. Imelda Guyton Hunt Ph.D

CHAPTER ONE

Introduction

From January 15 through February 16, 1992, *The Genius of Jazz: Toledo Celebrates Tatum* was held in Toledo, Ohio to pay tribute to Art Tatum. The distinguished participants were New Orleans educator and performer Ellis Marsalis; Indiana University Professor David Baker; Oberlin College President Frederick Starr; Obie-winning playwright Amiri Baraka; columnist and jazz critic Leonard Feather; Toledo native, pianist Stanley Cowell; and the program's national honorary chairman Billy Taylor. Writes Taylor, "Art Tatum was a genius whose mastery of time is still unmatched in solo jazz piano . . . He was unquestionably the quintessential jazz pianist."[1]

The recognition that Billy Taylor and others accorded Art Tatum that week was singularly appropriate. For most of his adult life, Tatum had been a dominant figure both for his technique and his original harmonics on the jazz piano. When he died at the age of

---

[1] Sally Vallongo, *The Genius of Jazz: Toledo Celebrates Tatum* program.

47, he had perfected the art of solo piano. His death did not mark the end of his influence, his reputation continuing to spread worldwide. However, in Toledo, as the jazz pianist Billy Taylor and others noted, there has been a lack of understanding and appreciation for Tatum's gifts.[2] This was the catalyst for *The Genius of Jazz: Toledo Celebrates Tatum* and this study.

Through oral interviews this study charts the early experiences of Tatum in Toledo from the perspective of his family, friends, and fellow musicians. Although Tatum remained a private man throughout his life, a compilation of his early life experiences as observed by peers may be useful to future generations of Toledoans, benefitting from the interviewees' stories of the twenties and thirties.

The primary focus of this study, however, is Art Tatum from his birth in 1909 until he left Toledo in 1932.[3] There are many reviews of Art Tatum's recordings and musical contributions to jazz, but there has been very little detailed work about his life in Toledo. Many people want to know where Tatum came from and what were his early experiences.

Most of the major works to date regarding Tatum have been written by people from outside the community. This study, however,

---

[2] Sally Vallongo, *The Genius of Jazz: Toledo Celebrates Tatum* program.
[3] Birth Certificate, Ohio Bureau of Vital Statistics, Columbus, OH.

provides a different focus. An additional benefit of this research is the comprehensive compilation of documentation of his life in Toledo, where Tatum lived out his first 23 years, prior to moving to New York City where he became recognized in the musical world for his musical genius. This study is based on interviews designed to illuminate Tatum's youth before becoming a famous musician. The interviews include information about his childhood, school experiences, family, church life, friends, and musical associates during his Toledo residency. Among the questions raised were: What was the source of his musicianship? And how did his parents influence his life and his music?

His life spanned decades which were crucial to the development of today's African American culture. Lawrence W. Levine writes in Black Culture and Black Consciousness that:

Emancipation brought educational, occupational, and spatial mobility and mobility enhanced acculturation. But underlying all the changes there persisted crucial residues of traditional culture which helped shape expressions in every sphere of black life . . . [4]

An examination of postbellum black religion and music would indicate these developments.[5]

---

[4] Lawrence W. Levine, Black Culture and Black Consciousness. Oxford University Press: London, 1977. 9, p. 155.
[5] Levine 155, 191.

Tatum's famous piano style developed in Toledo during the twenties and thirties, a time which has become known as the Jazz Age. This study lends credence to the argument that there is a correlation between national movements and local history during the Jazz Age. The arts movement of the Harlem Renaissance, a cultural movement that began with the articulations of African American intellectuals and artists of their recognition of African heritage, for instance, may be reflected in the oral history of Art Tatum's formative years. Many writers would agree that the proving ground for musicians is not the famous night spots that we are accustomed to hearing about in magazines such as Downbeat, but bars, and other black social gathering sites such as rent parties, jukes, and honky-tonks.[6] Art Tatum spent his early years in Toledo's bars, honky-tonks, and rent parties before going to New York where he received world recognition. He developed the Tatum style during this time of Toledo's cultural ferment. Art Tatum died[7] in 1956 of uremia.[8]

This book documents, from spoken sources, the life of Art

---

[6] Katrina Hazzard-Gordon, Jookin. Gordon has listed the various activities at these places and jazz was popular

[7] Death Certificate-California Department of Health Services, Sacramento.

[8] J. Dereck Jeffers and Moira Lerner, Harrison's Principles of Internal Medicine (New York: McGraw-Hill, 1983) 1612-1619. Uremia is the term generally applied to the clinical syndrome observed in patients suffering from profound loss of urinary function.

Tatum from 1909 until 1932. While there have been numerous scholars, such as Wilma Baum, who argue the validity of oral sources of history,[9] at best the life of the great Tatum can only be partially reconstructed from interviews with those who knew him. No original writings by Tatum exist today. Consequently, oral methodology remains the only available avenue to the reconstruction of his life. For instance, it is not known what Tatum experienced emotionally while honing his talents and developing his skills on the piano. Most scholarship relating to him can be gleaned only from other musicians who performed with him or who performed in Toledo during those same years. This submission, however, is not an examination of Tatum's musical style or the technical aspects of his piano genius, scholars such as Felicity Howlett and Joseph A. Howard have already explored these aspects of Tatum in their writings.[10] Rather, the focus here is reconstruction and enlightenment of his early formative years and musical background in Toledo.

Many spoken sources compiled in this volume are from people who had firsthand contact with Tatum. Other sources are derived from stories told to study informants by their parents and local business owners such as Rose Newton and Clifford Murphy (a

---

[9] David K. Dunaway and Willa K. Baum, Oral History. American Association for State and Local History: Tennessee, 1984. (xiii).
[10] Felicity Ann Howlett, "An Introduction to Art Tatum's Performance Approaches Composition, Improvisation, and Melodic Variation," diss., Cornell University, 1983.

tavern owner and musician). The ages of informants vary. Some younger contributors remember Tatum as an aspiring musician and recall his influence on them at an early age; while others, like Mayola Senior (age 77), remembers Tatum's first band and her husband Milton Senior's participation in it.

Methodology:

In her book, From Memory to History: Using Oral Sources in Local Historical Research, on reconstructing folk history from oral sources, Barbara Allen notes that the researcher should define a community's geographical and cultural boundaries in accordance with the concepts held by the people who lived there during the period under scrutiny.[11] She further explains that people's statements may differ sharply from those of outsiders. Taking cues from her suggestions, I have collected oral data from Tatum's Toledo contemporaries. The principal oral interviews for this book were collected between January 1992 and June 1993. Secondary sources, used for corroboration have been selected from John Cleveland's collected oral interviews, compiled in a 1983 videotape on Tatum.[12]

---

[11] Barbara Allen, From Memory to History: Using Oral Sources in Local Historical Research (Nashville: American Association of State and Local History, 1981) 19.
[12] John Cleveland's Private Collection. Copies of all interviews were made available to the author.

Interviews of Tatum's family are drawn from articles and Felicity Howlett's dissertation.

In these interview tapings, informants were asked to tell their story about Art Tatum. Those interviews are only slightly edited for the purpose of clarity. The character of the informants' words has been maintained. At the time of these interviews, Toledo celebrated a month-long, citywide celebration of the genius of Tatum. Most informants' memories had already been stimulated by the well-advertised and well-attended event before the interview. This celebration, triggering the memory of the informants, may have influenced their portrayal of Tatum as the publicized image. However, according to oral historian Tamara Hareven, "a sense of history does not depend on the depth of generational memory, but identity and consciousness, because they rest on the linkage of the individual's life history and family history with specific historical moments."[13]

This dissertation confirms that the people of Toledo who knew the young Tatum illuminate the life of the famous Art Tatum. Joan Russell, the owner of Murphy's Jazz Club in Toledo, states that "Tatum often said 'Everyone has a story to tell.'"[14] This study includes the collective stories that the people of Toledo have to tell

---

[13] Hareven 248.
[14] Joan Russell, personal interview, 20 March 1992.

about Tatum.

Taped interviews are grouped according to the informant's relationship to Tatum. Age and other characteristics of these informants vary. The informants range from those who have firsthand observations of Tatum, those who had personal interactions with him, and contemporaries who had conversations over the years with other members of the community about Tatum. Emphasis has been placed on taped interviews, corroboration with other documents (i.e., newspapers, journal articles), and visual sources (i.e., photographs, videotapes). This method makes useful the broad range of interviews used in this book: the accounts of personal experiences with Tatum, the family stories about Tatum, musicians' experiences who worked with Tatum, and those who came after Tatum. Similarly, the interviews permit the telling of the Toledo's past in the context of Tatum's life, and the emergence of the legend of Tatum within the community. Extraneous data not directly relating to Tatum, and pre-interview and post-interview chitchat have been edited from the transcribed interviews, as informants told their stories without interruption. Interviewer comments and questions served to clarify or expand a particular aspect of Tatum's life. The transcribed interviews, therefore, contain questions as well as the informants' narrations. The method employed in this scholarship is recommended by Allen and Willa K.

Baum in <u>Oral History: An Interdisciplinary Anthology</u>, for reconstructing history from oral sources.[15]

Selected documents that have already been published about Tatum are referenced because the validity of orally-communicated history relies upon the comparisons of such works with the taped interviews. Although there have been arguments about the reliability of human memory,[16] ethnohistorians have argued the veracity of orally-communicated history among American Indians, Africans, and South Asian groups. Allen mentions other tests, both internal and external, for determining the validity of oral sources.[17] She suggests that "each oral account be considered as truth as it is known by the informant. This allows that all informants' taped interviews are valid when the purpose is to obtain an accurate and revealing impression of people including Art Tatum, from those who knew or knew of him.[18] The methodology acknowledges that the incidental details revealed by informants in describing historical events and personalities has been embellished

---

[15] Willa K. Baum and David K. Dunaway, ed., <u>Oral History: An Interdisciplinary Anthology</u> (Nashville: American Association for State and Local History, 1984) 8.

[16] Louis Starr, "Oral History." <u>Oral History</u>. (American Association for State and Local History: Tennessee, 1984) 5.

[17] Tamara Hareven. "The Search for Generational Memory." <u>Oral History</u>, ed. Willa Baum and David K. Dunaway. (American Association for State and Local History: Tennessee, 1984) 248. Hareven defines generational memory as "memories which individuals have of their own families' history, as well as more general collective memories about the past."

[18] Allen 10-15.

or colored to make the incidents more memorable. Allen and other oral historians suggest a careful evaluation of the content of interview data.

When dealing with divergent accounts, it is important to examine the credibility of the individual informants for personal interests and biases, as well as bias found in written materials such as newspaper articles and editorials.[19] Identifying underlying biases of the taped interviews helps in maintaining the accuracy of the evaluation.

Informant Pool:

While the objectivity of any researcher is limited,[20] being an insider to the ethnic culture of Tatum and his contemporaries as well as being familiar with the overall community, its popular history, and cultural norms enabled the author to recognize such biases.

Drawing upon theatrical work within the Toledo community allowed the author additional contact with people in the arts community who were potential informants or who helped identify and make informants available.[21] The author's poetry performance

[19] Allen 3-24.
[20] Molefi Asante, The Afrocentric Idea (Philadelphia: Temple U. Press) 141.
[21] "Celebrating Tatum," a poetry and dance tribute to Tatum written and performed by Imelda Hunt, Tonya Steward, and Lindale Jones. This was part of the "The Genius of Jazz" Toledo Celebrates Tatum" 10 February 1992 at Murphy's Jazz Cafe. This

entitled "Celebrating Tatum" (performed in February 1992 at Murphy's Jazz Club during a month-long Tatum tribute) initiated contacts with other Toledoans, musicians, and scholars who have taken an interest in Tatum's work.

Written Resources Drawn Upon:

Allen recommends that there be corroboration from several sources: the material culture, tradition from continuation in the same area, tradition through ethnic group or racial groups, printed records, and accounts in regional historical literature.[22] Edrene Cole's 1967 Masters thesis, An Elementary School Instructional Unit for the Teaching of Blacks in Toledo Ohio[23] and LeRoy William's 1977 dissertation, "Black Toledo, Afro-Americans In Toledo, Ohio 1890-1930"[24] were used as background sources on Toledo's local history and its institutions.

---

month-long celebration of Art Tatum was presented by the Humanities Institute of the University of Toledo and the Toledo Museum of Art.
[22] Allen 28.
[23] Edrene Cole, "An Elementary School Instruction Unit for the Teaching of Blacks in Toledo Ohio," thesis, U. of Toledo, 1967, 1.
[24] LeRoy Williams, "Black Toledo, Afro-Americans In Toledo, Ohio 1890-1930," diss., U of Toledo, 1977.

Oral Resources Drawn Upon:

How Can I Keep From Singing: Pete Seeger offers a model for using oral documents as a source for writing unwritten folk and community history.[25]

Review of the Literature on Art Tatum:

James Lester, author of Too Marvelous for Words, covers the gamut of Tatum's life.[26]   Although he writes about Tatum in Toledo, his focus is on Tatum's musical talent from birth to his untimely death in California in 1956. His research leaves open some very intriguing gaps, such as Ella P. Stewart's role in Tatum's life. Stewart and her husband, acting as agents for Tatum, were responsible for Tatum's contract with Adelaide Hall, the singer with whom Tatum left Toledo in 1932.   This research addresses this period.   Felicity Ann Howlett, in An Introduction to Art Tatum's Performance Approaches: Composition, Improvisation, and Melodic Variation, analyzes Tatum's music and offers a method for approaching the gifts of Art Tatum in her 1983 dissertation.[27] Joseph

---

[25] Dunaway, How Can I Keep From Singing: Pete Seeger (New York: McGraw-Hill Book Company, 1981).

[26] James Lester, Too Marvelous for Words (New York: University of Oxford Press, 1994) 1-14.

[27] Howlett 1.

A. Howard provides in his Ph.D. dissertation The Improvisational Techniques of Art Tatum[28] an analytical discussion, graphic analysis, charts, and a discography. Arnold Laubich and Ray Spencer include in their book, Art Tatum: A Guide to his Recorded Music, indices of Tatum's published music as well as a discography.[29] Additionally, Tatum wrote a book called, Improvisation, No.2: Piano Interpretations of American's Outstanding Songs by Art Tatum.[30] John Cleveland's, The Tatum Legacy, is a 26-minute video with interviews of people and musicians, some of whom are now deceased, discussing the music of Art Tatum.[31]

Although Art Tatum has been discussed in other books examining the history of jazz (e.g., The Jazz Tradition, written by Martin Williams--a short history of jazz seen through the eyes of some of the important individuals of jazz such as King Oliver, Sara Vaughan, and Art Tatum), none have been entirely devoted to Tatum's life in Toledo.[32] These works contain information on the structure of Tatum's music and those events in Tatum's life that

---

[28] Joseph A. Howard, The Improvisational Techniques of Art Tatum, diss., Case Western Reserve, 1980, 5.

[29] Arnold Laubich and Ray Spencer, Art Tatum: A Guide to his Recorded Music (NJ: Scarecrow Press, 1982).

[30] Art Tatum, Improvisation, No. 2: Piano Interpretations of American's Outstanding Songs by Art Tatum (New York: Robbins Music Co., 1946).

[31] John Cleveland, The Tatum Legacy, videotape, prod., Toledo Public Library, 1983.

[32] Martin Williams, Jazz Masters in Transition: 1959-1969 (New York: MacMillan, 1970).

influenced his music after he left Toledo. Howlett offers in her chapter, "Portrait of The Man," anecdotes from interviews on the legend of Art Tatum. She describes Tatum's early recognition by other musicians, pointing to his uniqueness as a pianist in night spots and all-night competitions in Toledo. Howlett relies on Francis Williams, a childhood friend of Tatum, for an account of Tatum's early piano experiences.[33] (Williams did not recognize how good Tatum was until he went on the road and saw that other pianists could not line up with Tatum. His companionship with Tatum runs from marble games to all-night sessions in Toledo's after-hour clubs).

Howlett also tries to reconstruct the origin of Tatum's unique piano style and his undisputed genius, but she is hindered by the paucity of the research found on Tatum's early years. She argues that there should be one volume devoted entirely to his life off the piano stool. She notes that "confusion and contradiction concerning the facts of Tatum's personal life, education, and blindness characterize many articles that have been printed about him."[34] Since all of these events happened between 1909 and 1932, a study of Tatum in Toledo eliminates some of the confusion related to his blindness and early life. During the Art Tatum Conference in

---

[33] Howlett 44.
[34] Howlett 21.

February 1992, Arnold Laubich and others also note this gap in Tatum's history.

Arnold Laubich and Ray Spencer in their complete discography of Tatum's works, "Art Tatum: A Guide to His Record Music," have not included any biographical materials about his life Toledo residency. They wrote that:

Tatum was a genius. He changed the jazz piano. Not everyone plays like Tatum; few have the technique or courage to imitate him or to hazard a Tatum sound." Mary Lou Williams noted that Tatum "does all the things others try to do and can't . . . " Spellman observed that Tatum's keyboard mastery was complete, "he had absolute control. Most are influenced by him; all have to contend with his style and talent. If Tatum is not accepted fully he has to be rejected consciously. He cannot be ignored.[35]

Again, Tatum's music is emphasized, but little is discussed about the personhood and formative years of Tatum.

The aforementioned dissertations, biography, and discographies of his musical recordings and performances after 1932, include some biographical information none of which is devoted to the life of Art Tatum in Toledo. Such is the purpose of this study. The works of Howlett, Laubich, and Spencer allude to the paucity of information contained in written and oral sources and

---

[35] Laubich iii.

suggest that many of the articles, interviews, and other written works should be collected in a separate volume devoted to his life.[36] I would add that additional biographical information would serve to correct previously published inaccuracies regarding his life. For example, it was believed and had been published in most written sources that his birth year was 1910. Howlett writes in her dissertation that:

[the] biographical information is in such an elementary state that Tatum's birthdate has rarely appeared in print correctly . . . While doing biographical research on the west coast, Steve Ettinger [in 1949] checked Tatum's birth certificate and found that he was born on October 13, 1909 rather than as commonly assumed in 1910.[37]

This is, perhaps, the danger of studying the man and his music outside the contextual (Toledo) origin of his genius. What was it about the times and the environment that helped to influence the life and, concurrently, the music of Tatum and his contemporaries in Toledo? Howlett correctly calls our attention to the need for more

[36] Laubich xviii. They write in their preface that: the purpose of this book is to act as a catalyst for research, and to aid in the acquisition of materials to best and most fully enjoy the piano playing of the man we believe to be the most influential jazz pianist of our time. We have not included biographical information, anecdotes, lists of appearance, influences which Tatum had on others or they upon him, a bibliography, nor any detailed musical analysis.
[37] Howlett 9.

information about and clarification of the early years of Art Tatum's life.[38]

Historical Perspective of Toledo, Ohio

The Tatum Legend in Toledo

Contained within these interviews are accounts pertaining to Art Tatum's genius. Many people, including his family, can only guess at the origins of his piano genius. Many pianists reported, after hearing him for the first time, giving up the piano. Then there are the stories of his hand and how he acquired the fifth-finger spread, or "reach," which attributed to his ability to play "so much piano."[39] When trying to discover the validity or origins of legends such as this one, one finds that the story has been told so often or passed down so long ago that it has become popularly accepted as truth. Tatum is remembered legendarily in Toledo's after-hour establishments and among the night people as the musician who would come in from his regular night gig at a local club and play the piano nonstop until early morning, drinking beers that were lined up

---

[38] Howlett 9.
[39] Leonard Feather, "Leonard Feather Reviews 'Art Tatum': 20th Century Piano Genius," Los Angeles Times 18 May 1986, sec. C.: 58.

atop the piano. At least, so goes the legend of Tatum.

Tatum lived in Toledo during the time of the infamous regional Licavoli gang. This was a gang of mobsters from Detroit who allegedly ran the government and the streets of Toledo during prohibition, forcing a silence about their malfeasance among those who valued life. Even today, one often notes the glances of apprehension or the shift in mood whenever the Licavoli gang is mentioned. It is not always easy to get a community to talk that had once survived on their ability not to talk. Tatum reached manhood during the gang's influence on Toledo (1920-31) and began his musical career in their after-hours clubs and saloons.

Other legends describe the post-Toledo Tatum but point to characteristics that had their genesis in Toledo. Oscar Petersen said that "various people nationally alluded to Tatum's ability to use his left hand as a bass player."[40] Petersen, in a television interview with Andre Previn, said "I'd go to bed at night, and it haunted me (his first exposure to Tatum). It actually haunted me that someone could play piano that well [that way]." For two months after seeing Tatum, Petersen gave up the piano entirely.[41] Others have said that Tatum could sit down at any piano, regardless of missing keys, and "switch

---

[40] Oscar Peterson and Andre Previn, television interview hosted by Andre Previn, date and station unknown.
[41] Peterson and Previn.

keys or otherwise manage to perform as if there were nothing the matter.[42] Gene Rogers said, "I saw him [Tatum] play the piano, my legs turned to water, and I got sick. I had to go home. I came back after a couple of days."[43]

When one inquires as to the origin of Tatum's genius, there is surrounding him the same aura that is attached to a figure like the blues player, Robert Johnson. Born in 1911, Johnson received most of his fame and early experience in juke joints and ballrooms.[44] There is no one to tell us that Tatum stood at the crossroads and waited for the trickster to give him his talent, a legendary claim associated with the genius of the blues man, Robert Johnson. Tommy Johnson, who also left home scarcely able to play the blues like his brother Robert, describes the legend as follows:

Now if Tom was living, he'd tell you. He said the reason he knowed so much, said he sold hisself to the devil. I asked him how. He said, "If you want to learn how to play anything you want to play and learn how to make songs yourself, you take your guitar and you go to where a road crosses that way, where a crossroads is. Get there, be sure to get there just a little 'fore 12:00 that night so you'll

---

[42] Howlett 32.

[43] Gene Rodgers, discussion with Felicity Howlett, West End Cafe, New York City, 8 February 1982.

[44] Peter Guralnick, Searching for Robert Johnson (New York: Obelisk Dutton, 1989) 10-18.

know you'll be there. You have your guitar and be playing a piece there by yourself . . . A big black man will walk up here and take your guitar, and he'll tune it. And then he'll play a piece and hand it back to you. That's the way I learned to play anything I want.[45]

Son House, Robert Johnson's contemporary and blues singer, was convinced that Johnson had done the same thing, and undoubtedly, as Johnny Shines, a bluesman and another of Johnson's contemporaries, says "others were, too." One feels that the same type of legend is associated with Tatum's genius.

Art Tatum's Toledo:

Early in the twentieth century (1909) Tatum's parents, Mildred Heerston and Arthur Tatum, Sr., made their way from North Carolina to begin a new life in Toledo, Ohio. Shortly after their arrival Arthur Tatum, Jr. was born.[46] It has not been established why the young couple chose Ohio, but at the turn of the century many factors made Ohio attractive to southern black families migrating North. The fact that slavery had never been legalized in Ohio and that parts of Ohio had been stations in the Underground Railroad made for an

---

[45] Toledo Blade 14 July 1958.
[46] Toledo Blade 14 July 1958.

atmosphere conducive to a relatively peaceful settlement.[47] This enticed African Americans to settle in the area early. According to Edrene Cole, the 1860 census showed three hundred African Americans living in Toledo, and in 1910 Toledo had about 2,000 African Americans.[48] African Americans like the Tatums, who migrated from the south Atlantic states (Virginia, North Carolina, South Carolina), comprised 16.6% of the total black population and were the third largest group of African Americans who had migrated to Toledo.[49] They produced social institutions early, helping with the transitioning of newly arrived African Americans. In the last year of the civil war (1866), the Warren African Methodist Episcopal Church, an African American church, had been founded.[50]

Besides the Baptists, the Methodists were the only other denomination to license black preachers with any frequency. In mixed churches, too, there was tension between fellowship and slave status. In 1816 a separatist movement among black Methodists led by Richard Allen to the creation of the African

---

[47] Cole 1-3. Cole has documented the existence of the houses/routes used for the Underground Railroad in Toledo and surrounding areas and some of the participants, like African Americans David Adams, Joel Merkle and R.B. Hurd.

[48] Cole 2.

[49] Everette Johnson, "A Study of the Negro Families in the Pinewood Avenue District of Toledo, Ohio" (Survey conducted in 1923).

[50] E.L. Wheaton, "The Social Status of The Negro in Toledo, Ohio," diss., U of Toledo, 1927, 12. These earlier Africans were cooks, butlers, coachmen, waiters, maids, laundresses and some barbers, hairdressers, hotel and restaurant proprietors.

Methodist Episcopal Church in Baltimore.[51]

Toledo had already questioned the notion of segregated schools by 1909. In fact, the Jefferson Street school that Art would attend admitted "colored children" as early as 1880.[52] In 1927, blacks continued to progress in Toledo schools. According to a report of March 7, 1927 received from Superintendent Charles S. Meek of the Public Schools, "there were enrolled 147 Negroes in the public high schools and 1,574 in the grade schools of the city and at the University of Toledo the enrollments of Negroes were 21."[53]

However, it is important to remember that Arthur and Mildred Tatum would be looking to established families such as the Stewarts for direction and guidance.[54] If the Tatums came to Toledo in search of employment, there is evidence that African Americans in Toledo had a small advantage. The Tatums arrived in Toledo during the first tricklings of the Great Migration. The Tatum's early migration, nevertheless, was inspired by the same general concerns and problems associated with the mass movement of African Americans to the urban North from 1914-1923. A 1923 convention of African Americans held in Mississippi concluded that blacks, such

---

[51] Albert J. Raboteau, Slave Religion: "The Invisible Institution" in the Antebellum South, (Oxford: Oxford University Press, 1978) 204-8.
[52] Wheaton 12. Also in the interview with Arlene Tatum that is a part of this work she said that Tatum went to this school.
[53] Wheaton 15.
[54] See letter from Ella P. Stewart appended.

as the Tatums, were leaving Mississippi (and the South in general) because:

1) The Negro feels that his life is not safe in Mississippi; that his life may be taken with impunity at any time upon the slightest pretext or provocation by a white man, 2) The defeat of Southern representatives in Congress of the Dyer Anti-Lynching Bill has caused the Negro to believe that the South is irrevocably determined to perpetuate lynch law, mob violence, racial discrimination in economy, social and political matters, 3) The Negro has generally despaired of obtaining his rights as a citizen of this section, 4) While the law on its face is fair, when it comes to an application of that law to him, too often it is but a dead letter such a state and condition must ever remain just so long as he is denied the ballot.[55]

The Tatums and many other African American families would bring to Toledo their individual and collective experiences and aspirations.

Employment and Housing in Toledo, 1909-1932:

In order to understand Toledo at the time of Tatum's youth, an examination of the employment and housing of African

---

[55] Monroe Work, Negro Year Book, 1925-1926 (Tuskegee Institute: Negro Yearbook Publishing Co., 1927) 8.

Americans during this time follows, providing a general feel for Art Tatum's surroundings and the family's position in their community.

All of the reasons for the Tatum's migration are not known but according to Arlene, Art Tatum's younger sister, the Tatum's came to Toledo from North Carolina after hearing good things about Toledo from their relatives. Arthur, Sr. found lucrative employment almost immediately, suggesting he came looking for employment.[56] After arriving, Arthur, Sr. worked at the gas company. After being laid off, he worked in a foundry and the National Supply Company, one of the first refineries and drilling companies established after oil was found in Ohio in the 1800s, until his death.[57] He worked for 31 years at National Supply Company.[58]

According to statistics cited by Wheaton, a 1926 organizer of the local National Negro Business League called the "Negro Business League," in 1910 African Americans in Toledo were being employed in factories, foundries, railroad shops, building trades, public works, mercantile firms, and other industrial establishments.[59] He further showed that in 1910, 98% of African Americans in Toledo were unskilled. In 1923, more than 72.3% were

[56] Arlene Taylor, interview with John Cleveland, 6 November 1981.
[57] I. Hunt, personal telephone conversation, 9 September 1993
[58] Tana Porter, Toledo Profile: A Sesquicentennial History (Toledo: Lucas County Public Library, 1987) 7.
[59] Wheaton 20.

unskilled, 16.6% were semi-skilled and 11% were skilled class.[60] This indicates that the years between 1910-1923 marked a significant gain in the variety of employment for African Americans in Toledo. This would have some bearing on the type of economic opportunities the Tatums and other African Americans had at this time.

Everette Johnson, in "A Study of the Negro Families in the Pinewood Avenue District of Toledo, Ohio," writes that the major districts of the African American population in 1923 were sectioned around the major industries of Toledo rather than in one central location. These eight districts were the Hill Avenue District, the Canal District, the Pinewood District, the Canton Avenue District, the Yondota District, the Crystal District, the Summit Avenue District, and the Stickney Avenue District, differentiating Toledo from other major cities in that there was not a major concentration of African Americans in one area or one major "ghetto" that developed. One Toledoan, Clarence G. Smith, who arrived in Toledo in 1927 from Pittsburgh, favored Toledo over Pittsburgh because "Houses [in Pittsburgh were] perched on the side of a hill where most Negroes had to live."[61]

---

[60] Wheaton 27.
[61] Clarence G. Smith, Interview No. 11, Helen B. Kriner from the Toledo Public Library Oral Histories collection of the Afro-American Experiences in Toledo, 1976 November 10.

The conditions of these homes and the cost of rent in Toledo were much better than in Detroit and Chicago, a prime factor in he black migration to Toledo.[62] In 1923, Forester B. Washington found in a survey conducted by the Toledo Council of Churches that "27.6% of the Negro families investigated owned their own homes or were buying them.[63] Many houses outside those eight previously mentioned districts were shanties. These were dilapidated, rat and vermin-infested shanties. Outside the city limits there existed an area known as the Airline Junction Quarters which consisted of one hundred two-room shanties which were rented by the railroad to African American employees.[64] However, the Airline Junction quarters seemed to be the exception rather than the rule in Toledo.

Although African Americans were limited in their selection of neighborhoods, they did have several districts to choose from, depending on the individual family's income. There was little residential separation between the nationalities/races--Irish, Polish, Italians, and African Americans lived in the same neighborhood without controversy until the twenties when people began

---

[62] Wheaton 36.
[63] Wheaton 1.
[64] Wheaton 37, 20. Although this might seem to contradict Smith's statement that the condition of housing is relative, it depends upon who is making the assessment, why, and when. However, to get a complete picture of what the housing conditions were in Toledo during the time of Tatum, I considered all of the details about the various African American districts essential.

competing for jobs, according to Geraldine Moreland, a resident of Toledo during the twenties.[65]   Mrs. Moreland, a seamstress, hairdresser, and later a Realtor, had been associated with many of Toledo's underworld personalities during prohibition. She would have been admitted into places that perhaps others would not. African Americans during this period had a variety of experiences dependent upon their occupation and social status. Clarence G. Smith, for an example, stated his disagreement with Mrs. Moreland:

Across the street from where I lived, they put in a whole row of houses you know, just tied on to one another . . . And those are still there [in 1978]. The Negroes were not admitted in those houses when they were new because I remember playing with the white boys who lived across the street . . . Then on the left of where I lived there was a row of houses --the same kind.[66]

He, obviously, was not as privileged as Mrs. Moreland. Johnson also argues that there was a residential separation, like in other cities, and African Americans were admitted into these communities after the Polish, Irish or other ethnic groups had lived in the homes and were ready to move out.

Other lines of segregation also existed. Toledo's housing

---

[65] Geraldine Moreland, interview from the Toledo Public Library Oral Histories collection of the Afro American Experience in Toledo, 18 April 1978.
[66] Smith, <u>Afro-American Experiences in Toledo</u>.

separation seemed to have occurred among African Americans themselves. The separation was along the lines of long-established families and newcomers. Johnson attributes this to the African American system of status which says that "the length of time in the city is the measure of fitness for leadership, and the judgment of the masses rests in the hands of this minority."[67] These established families were also entrusted with overseeing the conduct of the newcomers from the South. It is important to note here that these longtime Northern families helped shape the development of African American music, as well as religion and culture. If the newcomers were to assimilate, they would have to concede some of their southern ways. Hence, the established families became the gatekeepers of African American culture in the North by defining acceptable music, dance, and social conduct.[68]

Another area that needs to be considered in this survey of African American housing during Tatum's time is the Canton District. This district, known then as the "tenderloin area" was expanded in

---

[67] Johnson 1.

[68] Kathy J Ogen, The Jazz Revolution: Twenties America and the Meaning of Jazz (New York: Oxford Press, 1989) 113-4. When New Orleans and other "hot" style musicians moved North, their status as newcomers produced new objections to jazz. Willie "the Lion" Smith felt the average Negro family did not allow blues" precisely because they wanted to distance themselves from the South. In many cities to which southern blacks came before and after World War I, inter-racial conflicts developed over the behavior and lifestyles of the newcomers. More established blacks upbraided newcomers for attracting negative attention to the black community."

the twentieth century to included Erie, Jackson, Beech, Ontario, and Canton streets. This was where African Americans residing inside the city limits at the bottom of the economic hierarchy, lived. It was also a district that was singled out for its social problems. Patrolled by Edward Ashby, the city's lone African American police officer, the Canton District was created from the racially-oriented precincts of blacks and whites in the city.[69] It was in this area that the dragnet system (where an individual could be arrested on suspicion) was instituted to help reduce crime.[70] The reasons for the high crime and vagrancy, according to one city official, was the deplorable housing conditions.

Most people, during these early years of Toledo's development, resided in housing close to where they worked. In 1929 the majority of the African American population worked at the Willys Overland plant and lived in the Stickney District, while some African Americans who worked for New York Central Railroad lived adjacent to the Round House and shops in the Hill Avenue District.[71] The Pinewood District, where Art Tatum stayed with his family in the early twenties and thirties, was the primary residential area of the

---

[69] Williams 96.
[70] Williams 96.
[71] Johnson 1.

African American middle class.[72] Johnson's study found that most homes were lighted by electricity, others by "primitive" lamplights. In one block outside toilets were being used.[73] This suggests that African American housing in the Pinewood District was below the standards of the time.

The Tatum family's first house was a two-story, three-bedroom dwelling at 1123 City Park. Apparently the Tatums lived somewhat better than the average African American homeowner in this district during this time. According to Arlene Tatum Taylor, her parents came to Toledo with money of their own to purchase the house in which Arthur, Jr. was born. Later, when the Tatums purchased their home on Mitchell Street, they also bought an adjacent lot and built a park in which their children and others from the neighborhood played. They named it Tatum Park. A duplex presently occupies the site.[74] Also living on Mitchell Street were the young Tatum children's two aunts on their father's side of the family, one a gospel singer.[75] Both aunts continued to live in the same house until their deaths in 1992. Arthur, Sr. seemed to have taken

---

[72] John Rinehart 52. See map. Although this map was designed in 1939, the location of the various dwellings are important for this study of Tatum's neighborhood. There are poolrooms located on Indiana and Collingwood approximately two blocks up the street from the Tatum family home. This would be within walking distance for Tatum.
[73] Johnson 1.
[74] Cleveland, The Tatum Legacy.
[75] See-Church Membership List.

the quality of his family's lifestyle seriously. Conditions in Toledo were favorable to achieving a comfortable lifestyle. The Tatum family was not considered poor within the African American community. Rather, Arthur, Sr.'s position in the church and his ability to meet the required economic status necessary to reside in the Pinewood District suggest that the family was in many ways a member of the middle class.

The black community had increasing occupational and self-employment categories as indicated by a listing in the 1926 Charter of the Local Negro Business League: ten tailor shops, six ice and coal dealerships, four poolrooms, three real estate offices, two sign painters, three soft drink parlors, three trucking houses, seven grocery stores, three hotels, six insurance offices, nine barber shops, four auto repair shops, two carpenters and contractors, two taxi service stations, two undertaker establishments, one cement contractor, one landscape gardener, one milliner and flower maker, one photographer, two plumbers, one printer, one electrician, one window shade manufacturer, one lamp shade manufacturer, one bric-a-brac manufacturer, two painters and decorators, one drug store, and one fish market. The professions included two pharmacists, seven physicians, three dentists, one chiropodist, five lawyers and seventeen ministers.[76]

African American women generally were employed as domestic help. Mildred Tatum was no exception; she worked as a domestic in Ottawa Hills.[77] Wheaton writes that some women were maids, stockroom workers and elevator operators in department stores. Others were employed in pool halls and rag factories. There were three black women employed by the county as stenographers and three employed by the Board of Education as teachers in the public school.[78]

Although these years of urbanization in Toledo show a large increase in other ethnic populations, the number of African Americans arriving in the flourishing Toledo area was much slower in comparison to the white ethnic groups. Given the percentage of African Americans in Toledo, racial biases with labor unions similar to those experienced by African Americans in other cities, and the desirability of factory jobs, Arthur, Sr.'s job at National Supply Company was in all likelihood, highly desirable among African Americans and other ethnic populations.

---

[76] Wheaton 47-48. Wheaton helped organize the local chapter.
[77] See the Harold Payne Interview.
[78] Wheaton 21.

Toledo's Popular Culture in the Twenties:

In 1925 Toledo had an estimated population of 287,380.[79] A flourishing metropolis, Toledo could boast about its cultural resources, which there is every reason to believe Tatum partook of. In This Week in Toledo, a weekly magazine, an unidentified writer once observed that many of the newly released films came to Toledo before they went to major cities such as Chicago and Detroit. The columnist went on to note that Toledo had "a fine old stage tradition, still retains its well-earned reputation for super-acute criticism."[80] During the twenties Toledo had several forms of entertainment: movies, vaudeville, musical concerts, as well as thriving "legitimate" theater (a term coined for stage productions such as "Hallelujah"). Toledo also had a track for greyhound racing and golf courses, with golf approaching the same popularity as baseball.

As a result of the industrial revolution, a new lifestyle of the twenties was clearly emerging that would be distinguished as the introduction of leisure-time activities. Leisure time thrived with the help of newspapers and periodicals. In fact, the Toledo Topics, published from December 1925 through November 1929, reads like

---

[79] Wheaton 32.
[80] Toledo Topics Nov. 1927: 1.

the Great Gatsby. The monthly magazine, originally devoted to golf, had articles covering movies, books, New York, Paris, sports, fashion, and Toledo gossip. The Toledo Topic featured monthly columns entitled "Chitchat of the Theaters," "Where to Go and What to See," "The New York Theater," "The Iconoclast in New York," "Town Talk," "Musical Moments," and feature articles. In the column "Where to Go and What to See," the theaters were classified into 'legitimate theater' and 'motion pictures.' The legitimate theaters listed in the November 1927 issue of Toledo Topic were the "Place" and "B.F. Keith's," advertising both vaudeville and feature motion pictures.[81] The motion picture theaters listed were Loew's Valentine and the Pantheon. The restaurants in "Where to Dine" were The Secor and the Bay Shore Inn, both with house orchestras. Prior to the publication of the Toledo Script, published by W. E. Barnett in 1943, print materials carried black news and announcements.

The Harlem Renaissance was in its prime at this time with related announcements appearing in Toledo's media. The Harlem Renaissance, a cultural movement begun when African American intellectuals and artists articulated personal recognition of their African heritage, resulted in recognition and mainstreaming of various African American artists into American popular culture. The list included Langston Hughes, Claude McKay, Gene Toomer, Counte

---

[81] Toledo Topics Nov. 1927: 2-3.

Cullen, Zora Neal Hurston, Nella Larson and James Weldon Johnson. As was noted earlier, Harlem, "the capital of the Negro world," was in the 1900s a place that recently had been vacated by Dutch Americans and left to the African Americans. In Harlem you could find rent parties; dances like the Charleston (with its origins in a West African Ashanti ancestor dance[82]), the Black Bottom, and the Lindy Hop (named after Charles Lindbergh); the Lafayette Theater; straightened hair; and bleaching cream beauty parlors; and jook joints. During this era jooks underwent the transition from boxes (guitars) to pianos. Zora Neale Hurston exclaimed that "Pianos soon came to take the place of the boxes, and now player-pianos and Victrola are in all of the jooks."[83] Although this was a movement that took place primarily in New York's Harlem, there was an impact of the Harlem Renaissance on the African American community in Toledo and on Art Tatum.

Black (folk) art was referred to as low brow art. Harry Shaw, in his introduction to Perspectives of Black Popular Culture makes the argument that "if . . . art is distinctly Black and popular (that is of the folk), it is also distinctly American."[84] The monthly magazine Toledo Topic provides an in-depth look at the popular culture of

---

[82] Harry Shaw, ed., Perspectives of Black Popular Culture, (Bowling Green State University Popular Press, 1990) 4.
[83] Zora Neale Hurston, I Love Myself (New York: The Feminist Press, 1979) 152.
[84] Harry Shaw 1.

Toledo during the twenties. Although the magazine did not market to African Americans, it is helpful for gauging Toledo's cultural climate and for discerning those activities Tatum could have been exposed to during the Jazz Age twenties, Tatum's formative years. A close examination of the magazine reveals the types of theatrical entertainment that was available in Toledo during the twenties.

The movie houses showcased vaudeville, feature movies and live theater on stage, some of which was African American. The March 1930 issue of the Toledo Topics carried a Loews' Valentine theater advertisement of the first all-Negro, talking, drama-history, "Hallelujah," calling it Dramatic! Weird! Haunting![85] "Hallelujah" was MGM's answer to the popular twenties Negro dramatic films. According to Gary Null Black Hollywood: The Black in Motion Pictures, these films seldom deviated from the stereotypical images that Hollywood maintained of the African American. In "Hallelujah" the African American images that dominated the film were of "the savage brute and the humble and subservient buffoon."[86]

References also were made to "Africana," the Ethel Waters' black musical show on Broadway, in the Toledo Topics monthly feature "New York Theater." Writer Watson C. Cady commented

[85] Toledo Topics Feb. 1927: 2.
[86] Gary Null, Black Hollywood: The Black in Motion Picture (New Jersey: Citadel Press, 1975) 36.

that "the negro is born with an instinct for it [dancing] and . . . if they would just let Ethel Waters strut her stuff they [the cast of "Africana"] would have little or nothing to worry about."[87] Many other references were made in this magazine that not only gave some indication of the cultural life of Toledo but also revealed a certain attitude the magazine held regarding the African American in general. There were, for example, many references made which were condescending about African American dialect. Although these were not in every issue, they were written without restraint as if matter of fact and subject to no one's scrutiny.[88]

Toledo press seems to have been notorious for its negative assessment of African Americans. LeRoy Williams writes in his dissertation that the treatment of African Americans in the Blade, a local newspaper, was one of the first concerns that the Toledo

---

[87] Watson C. Cady, "New York Theater," Toledo Topics November 1927: 21. Watson goes on to say that " the audience clamored long and hard for her old classic, "Shake That Thing," and, " . . . after managing to calm them, she consented, and said with a grin, "Land sakes! Ah thought yo' all would appreciate higher things!"
[88] Toledo Topics March 1929: 22. The following is a poem from that issue:
PLANTATION DRINKING SONG
De ladies in de palour.
Hey, come a rollin' down
A-drinkin' tea an coffee.
Good-mornin, ladies all!
De gemmen in de kitchen,
Hey come a rollin' down!
A-drinkin' brandy, toddy,
Good-mornin', ladies all!

Chapter of the NAACP addressed when formed in 1916 by local leaders Albertus Brown, Charles Cottrill, and Della Fields.[89] Williams reminds us that Toledo's popular culture was acknowledged by whites, but often their assessment of blacks left much to be desired by the African American community. Often this is the problem with an etic study of culture and community.

Many of the Harlem Renaissance writers' book reviews were included in the Toledo Topic's monthly feature, "Leafings." In the March 1928 issue some of the books reviewed were considered to be "race" novels, such as Jessie R. Fausset's Plum Bun and Wallace Thurman's The Blacker the Berry.[90] The novels that were highly recommended were novels about Harlem's social scene, like Banjo

[89] Williams, "Black Toledo, Afro-Americans in Toledo, Ohio, 1890-1930," 211. Toledo's NAACP also responded to one of the earliest national assaults on racism in the movie industry, "The Birth of a Nation." This movie condoned Klan activities throughout America. The Toledo chapter had 500 members and three mass rallies between 1916 and 1917.
[90] "Leafings," Toledo Topics March 1928: 10. The reviews of these two "race" novels also confirm the attitude that was popular among white journalists and socialites of Toledo during this time. The review read as follows:

> Two more of a veritable flood of "race" novels from the pens of colored folk. Neither of these is especially remarkable, the theme of each being stated rather well in this quotation from the latter [The Blacker the Berry] "we are all living in a totally white world, where all standards of the white man, and where almost invariably what the white does is right, and what the black man does is wrong, unless it is presented by something a white man has done." (Both books are good, of their type, but there's a bit too much propaganda in them.)

and Home to Harlem by Claude McKay.[91] In Toledo's African American community writers like Langston Hughes visited Toledo's social scene lecturing to African American clubs, suggesting that their popularity went beyond New York to other American cities and, more importantly, to the African American communities which they wrote about. Hughes often used jazz as the cultural backdrop of his novels, adding to the growing intellectual controversy that surrounded jazz music's social and cultural impact on American life.[92]

Alain Locke writes that nowhere in the history of humankind has any race been more culturally esteemed and imitated but so socially rejected than the Negro in America.[93] In the midst of the acknowledgment of Toledo Topic and other Toledo journalists of the accomplishment of black Americans in the arts there still existed conditions which Locke refers to as the "social rejection of blacks." Toledo's African Americans established a community of their own. Williams writes that "apart from the activities of the city's Empire Theater, black residents faced an almost total exclusion from other

---

[91] Toledo Topics March 1928: 10.

[92] Thomas Vines, "Black Women of the Nation," Mott Branch Library, Toledo, February 1993. This photo exhibition has a picture of Langston Hughes in Toledo with a women's group. Although there is no date, the exhibitor approximates the time of the photo to be in the early twenties.

[93] Alain Locke, Sounds of Blackness, From Africa to America, 1994.

areas of the city's life in the 1920s."[94] The nature of African American entertainment presented at the Empire Theater was the black counterpart to the white minstrel tradition with African Americans playing roles like "Shufflin' Sam from Alabam," "Shuffling Along," and "Lucky Sambo."[95] Also according to Williams other entertainment available to the African American in the Toledo community consisted of African American touring groups such as the "Seven Eleven" and the "Rang Tang Clowns," a black carnival sponsored by civic leaders at St. Paul A.M.E. Zion Church in July 1922, and a Negro National League baseball team called the Toledo Tigers who played for both blacks and whites at Toledo's Swayne Field.[96] This entertainment also exposed more blacks and whites to jazz music. Other African American actors and actresses listed in the Toledo Blade in the early twenties were Sam Cook, Garland Howard, Evon Robinson, May Brown, Eleanora Wilson, Bessie Sims, Lee Whipper, and Eddie Gray.[97]

In the Toledo Topics black images were further stereotyped by such events as an annual gala with pictures of whites attending in black face. What made events like these popular were the images that whites had of African Americans. Katy Ogen, in The Jazz

---

[94] Williams 270.
[95] Williams 269.
[96] Williams 269.
[97] Toledo Blade 3 July 1922 and Toledo Blade 1 and 5 May 1923.

Revolution: Twenties America and the Meaning of Jazz, cites that the

" . . . exotic primitivism associated with African Americans became more popular in mass culture as whites were encouraged to liberate themselves from over civilization."[98] Black vaudeville and minstrelsy created an image or expectancy of African American entertainers and entertainment.[99]

While these images of the African American were being formed in the mass media, Ethel Water's singing in "Africana" helped spread the popularity of the jazz music of the age. Other forms of popular entertainment, like "the Jazz Singer," which opened at the

---

[98] Katy Ogen, The Jazz Revolution: Twenties America and the Meaning of Jazz, (New York: Oxford University Press, 1989) 151. Ogen argues that "white writers like Van Vechten did not often experiment with jazz performance as an alternative language. Most often they used jazz milieus as settings or developed the idea that primitivistic jazz could liberate over civilized whites. Primitivism was an escape from identity for these writers, not the exploration of personal and racial pride that it had been for black writers in the Harlem Renaissance. Jazz performance remained a central focus of these white artistic experiments with the primitive, nonetheless, because white readers believed jazz performance could transmit the values of a simpler past into the furious present. The music emerged once again as a passageway--in this case, into the exotic world of black culture."

[99] Ogen 75. Ogen also argues that "black vaudeville, minstrelsy, and other kinds of staged performances had prepared white audiences for the kind of acts [found in New York City night spots] . . . the persistence among whites of stereotypes about black entertainment may have trapped both blacks and whites in roles that were not "authentic" but staged. In these cases, jazz performances became part of a contrived tradition." Music scholars and critics have often mentioned Tatum's genius at after-hours and parties. They often call our attention to the difference between the recorded Tatum and the live Tatum being much more superb. Perhaps the explanation is the same. The Tatum of the after-hours and cutting contests was in the presence of his peers and friends and having fun. He would have been without the artificial exceptions of the white supper club's audience and radio listeners.

Toledo's Vita-Temple Theater in 1928, starring Al Jolson reintroduced Toledoans to the jazz music previously heard played by Art Tatum in local settings. Radio also contributed to the rapid dissemination of jazz. In 1921 Toledo's first commercial radio station, WTAL, began broadcasting from the Navarre Hotel.[100] Later in 1928, Tatum performed for this station whose call letters were subsequently changed to WSPD. Bob Doerschuk writes in Keyboard Magazine an article entitled "An Art Tatum Biography" that:

He [Tatum] was also making a regional impact over the radio; in 1928 or '29, as a result of his performance on an amateur program, WSPD radio in Toledo hired him to play between Ellen Kay's daily shopping hints to household wives. Soon he had a 15-minute show of his own, which ran five days a week for more than two years and was eventually picked up for national broadcast by the old NBC Blue Network (now ABC).[101]

In 1928, the height of the Jazz Age, Tatum was 19 years old. Kathy Ogen writes that although the roots of jazz were in live performance, technological developments after 1900 made it possible to preserve and transmit black music to audiences far removed from the performer.[102] Likewise, Tatum would have been

---

[100] Porter 7.
[101] Bob Doerschuk, "An Art Tatum Biography," Keyboard Magazine, October 1981: 22.
[102] Ogen 87.

able to develop his famous style because these technological developments made the performances of other jazz artists such as Fats Waller and James P. Johnson available to him as a musician in his early childhood. Likewise, the movies and the music which formed the cultural milieu of the Jazz Age would have been part of Tatum's youthful Toledo experience.

According to Blade reporter Seymour Rothman, during his [Tatum's] Toledo years Art stayed very close to the black community. While white musicians came to the Waiters and Bellmans Club, an after-hours club on Indiana Avenue, to jam until dawn, there wasn't much mixing of the races outside."[103] Clubs and after-hours made up one aspect of both social and cultural trends of the Jazz Age, and were accountable to Prohibition.

Prohibition set the stage for an atmosphere which produced places such as Waiters and Bellmans and the Blue Lantern, where whites and blacks mixed socially. Harry R. Illman writes in his book Unholy Toledo that:

A new underworld personality of twentieth-century origin plagued American cities at the end of the First World War. The prejudices of the previous decades were forgotten. A kind of madness followed. There was reckless abandon in the roaring years of the Charleston and jazz, of the newly rich thirsting for

---

[103] Seymour Rothman, "Art Tatum's Toledo Years," Toledo Blade 30 June 1985: 12.

entertainment and amusement, of negro singers like Bessie Smith, of prohibition and a frantic, almost maniacal, interest in sports. The age of the rumble seat, plastic surgery and short hair with Marcel waves and the motion pictures had arrived.[104]

This would have a significant impact on Art Tatum (See Chapter IV).

Harold Payne, also one of the local musicians, performed with the young Tatum. According to Rothman, "Tatum and Payne were in demand, playing anywhere there was a piano, bootleg liquor, and a chance for tips, in places like La Tabernilla, Chateau La France, Chicken Charlie's, Darfey's, the Blue Lantern, and spots long forgotten."[105] Another of Tatum's companions, Harry Gregory, recalled that even as a child Tatum was famous for his piano and played in all kinds of places and he played in at least one of them out of fear. Gregory recalled that:

We were walking down 22nd Street and a guy came out and told us to come in and play the piano. It was a white boot joint. He [Art] really didn't want to play. The piano was way out of tune, but we were led to believe that the spot was run by Licavoli gangsters, so Art kept his mouth shut and played.[106]

---

[104] Illman 1.
[105] Rothman, "Art Tatum's Toledo Years" 12.
[106] Rothman, "Art Tatum's Toledo Years" 12.

Musically, Tatum's fame had already been established. How and why this occurred can be attributed to the times and also to Tatum's style. Arnold Laubich and Ray Spencer wrote, "Tatum is the most articulate representative of the tradition formed from the merging of ragtime, Dixieland and blues piano into stride and from there into and through the piano developments of the swing era."[107] The times that permitted the flourishing of the after-hours clubs also were the formative years for Tatum. It was during these times that Tatum grew to become a man and mature into the musician who later would receive worldwide acclaim.

Toledo offered many of the opportunities that Harlem did. Certainly the popular movies of the day came to Toledo and there were the "respectable [Black] night spots" like the Chateau de France and La Tabernilla listed in the Toledo Topics. The fashions, the large entertainment establishments, the underworld, and the availability of new media technology suggest that the name "Little New York" was an appropriate nickname for Toledo. Toledo also had Art Tatum. Felicity Howlett remarks that:

Word gradually spread among musicians that there was a young talent emerging, worthy of the best challenges and all-night competitions. By that time the musicians were seeking out Tatum at Val's, one of his favorite Cleveland spots, or making special trips

---

[107] Laubich and Spencer vii.

to the Toledo area to hear him play . . . [108]

This phenomenon is discussed later in Chapters IV and V.

Although whites were willing to listen and enjoy the musical talents of Tatum and other African American performers, Toledo had a distinct color line.[109] Williams writes that "beyond the contacts Reverend S. W. Warr made with white ministers with the Council of Churches, most black Toledoans continued to conduct their social and religious activities within a largely all black world."[110]

Prohibition, Crime, and the Licavoli Days:

Because drinking was "illegal" and due to the unfavorable role that Toledo's local government played, Harry R. Illman's book, Unholy Toledo, had received mixed reviews from Toledoans. The book is out-of-print and librarians in the local history department of the Toledo Lucas County Public Library remind clients of its poor documentation. Although Illman's book reflects the criminal and amoral view of city government, there seems to be no inaccuracies in the story Illman tells of his connection with Toledo's history and the underworld. Many of this study's informants recall Toledo's gangsters and local politicians. They tell a story similar to Illman's.

---

[108] Howlett 19.
[109] Williams 66.
[110] Williams 268.

The cover of Illman's book begins:

Ohio, beginning in 1868 with the election of Grant, to President, all were Republican. Every administration was marked with corruption. Running for Governor of that state was equated with running for president. Ohio was a hotbed of political intrigue and machinations. Ohio set the example for the rest of the states.[111]

Melvin M. Belli also writes in his introduction to Unholy Toledo that:

We knew that circa the Prohibition era, Kansas City was an oasis and sanctuary for fugitives. Regardless of their record or where they were "wanted," no one would bother them. But Toledo's similar history in this regard is not well known. It is now documented and delightfully told in this book.[112]

Illman addresses the influence that the government had in the corruption of labor and vice in the city. From the beginning industries received laws favorable to the employee, such as the Workmen's Compensation Act of 1911. Illman reminds us that after prohibition money had to be found somewhere so it was found in labor and labor racketeers. Pool halls, gambling joints, and drinking establishments were mostly owned by a Detroit mobster who

---

[111] Illman jacket cover.
[112] Illman v.

immigrated to Toledo and led by mobsters from The Purple Gang.[113] The fear this gang instilled compared to the word 'Mafia.' It is important to note that many of this study's informants still showed the shadow of what that fear was like. Casey Jones, for example, said the following:

That was the kind of life during that period of time in Toledo. I remember I used to live around Belmont and Collingwood. It was the days of all the gangsters and I used to see them guys out shooting up and down the street and we sat there and looked at them. Toledo was known for a gangster's hang out.[114] It was a town that if you committed crimes in other cities if you came to Toledo the rules that you played by were if you did nothing while you were in Toledo, nobody would bother you. Let's say you were a gangster and you did all of your stuff in Chicago, the rule was when you came to Toledo you did nothing and you were protected. We used to call it a gangster's hang out, that's the terms we used in our day.[115]

When asked questions about the gangsters some

---

[113] Illman 1.

[114] Beverly Shadie, "Purple Gang," Montage November 1993: 8. Thomas "Yonnie" Licavoli was invited by Toledoan, Flip Sulkin to share in the lucrative bootlegging activity along the concealed coastline of Lake Erie. Within two years, the lust for control gave rise to at least a dozen murders . . . The tough Detroit criminals who infiltrated this area called the "Purple Gang" . . . was similar to that of the original Chicago mobsters." Although there is some question about documentation of the material in the book, a complete story about these activities which Casey discusses in the interview can be found in Unholy Toledo written by Harry R. Illman.

[115] An Interview with Casey Jones.

informants remained silent. Such interviewees had difficulty disclosing information because previously such silence ensured their safety and continued existence. This tradition of verbal restraint has continued in the African American community since the days of slavery.

The Purple Gang terrorized Toledo from the early days of prohibition until they were stopped in 1931. Public outrage brought Prosecuting Attorney Frazier Reams to wage an all-out war against organized crime.[116] Not all African Americans, however, distanced themselves from the gangsters and their world. In fact, some found creative ways to profit from their lifestyle. Grace Moreland, a local woman who made money by making loans to local gamblers as well as sewing shirts for them, also opened a beauty shop to service the local women who operated and worked in the after-hours. She remembers them as the clientele who could most afford her services. According to Moreland, the local ladies-of-the-night, gangsters, gamblers, and mobsters were more generous and honest than the average church-going person.[117] Also Charlie's Chicken Shack (also referred to as Chicken Charlie's), an African American nightspot where Tatum performed operated by an African American

---

[116] Beverly Shadie 9.
[117] Geraldine Moreland Interview. As previously mentioned Mrs. Moreland was also a Realtor and owned rental property in Toledo.

named Johnnie Crocket, was a place where many gang members visited and conducted their business.

Even if the average African American did not have direct contact with the gangsters, their lives were affected indirectly by their presence in Toledo. For instance, many of the labor wars and power plays waged by the city officials and local labor unions and often controlled by the gangsters, affected African Americans who worked in the unskilled factory jobs. Selling a gangster-owned newspaper became a highly dangerous profession. African Americans were known to be newsboys during this time.[118] There is unconfirmed indication that Tatum also sold newspapers. Tatum's breaking of prohibition law by consuming alcohol is also documented in many places. Most revealing about Tatum during prohibition is an interview with his childhood friend Francis Williams who recalls that,

[He] loved to drink! In Prohibition, he was drinking like hell. Everything! We could get the bad whiskey that was being made then because the next state, Indiana, was the alkie center. Cleveland was the sugar center. All kinds of whiskey was being made, and then there were the bootleggers who were bringing in good whiskey from Canada. They were driving right across the ice on Lake Erie. Truckloads of good whiskey but good Scotch from abroad. However,

---

[118] Elder R., personal interview, 12 May 1993.

we drank everything. Oh, brother, what we use to do.

Art would start out on Saturday night. I'd stick with him until eight o'clock Sunday morning, come home, eat some raw coffee beans so my mother couldn't smell my breath, and drive my mother to church. I'd get a bit of sleep and rejoin Art on Sunday afternoon. He'd never stopped. I would leave him about five o'clock on Monday morning . . . Art would still be going Monday morning. He hadn't slept a wink. All he was doing was playing and drinking. We were just playing for tips. We'd start in one house and get whatever we could there and then go on to the next house. While Jimmy Davis would be playing, Art and I would be drinking, and maybe there would a few tips. The girls would say, "Give the kids something." After Jimmy Davis would play, I'd play. And Jimmy and Art would be drinking. Then Art would start playing and Jimmy and I would get drunk.[119]

Not only was Tatum's love of liquor affected by prohibition but his employment potential was also influenced by the increased number of locations for the consumption of bootleg alcohol. As previously mentioned, Tatum and Harold Payne played some gigs out of fear. The new owners of these lucrative speakeasies needed performers. Often Toledo's night clubs and cabarets were owned by men with criminal connections.

---

[119] Francis Williams, discussion with Felicity Howlett, 1 July 1975.

Summary:

In the 1920s Toledo was a progressive town for whites. The effects trickled down to the African American community in the form of jobs and small business ownership, allowing blacks to sustain some forms of entertainment. This period coincided with the development of Tatum's phenomenal talents.[120] Toledoans were familiar with the arts and music scene in Harlem, and in particular, the African American scene. Some Harlem activities spilled over to Toledo. The local after-hours, rent parties, and musical joints frequently found Europeans enjoying the music and nightlife of African Americans. Although Tatum played at fine European local night spots and dinner clubs in Toledo, it is highly unlikely that he would have been welcomed as a patron. Toledo's African Americans seemed to have established a community of their own. James Lester writes in <u>Too Marvelous for Words</u>, that " . . . it seems clear that Tatum grew up among stable people and was part of a family and

---

[120] Shaw 5. Shaw writes that: carving out a wholesome, health environment has also been the endeavor of that part of Black popular culture associated with health practices . . . Black recreation has provided an escape from not only the pressures of the work-a-day world but also the reality that historically segregation has most often barred Blacks from the outlets of fun and frivolity open to the public.

community with a settled lifestyle."[121] During the Jazz Age, Tatum's reputation as a piano player began to spread and other musicians coming to Toledo began to search for Tatum in its night spots.

The focus of this inquiry is to place Tatum within the context of Toledo. Other scholars have not addressed his Toledo origins. James Lester and other biographers believe that Toledo was an unusual place in which to find someone of Tatum's genius. Others, unaware of the area's history, have made the same assumption. This study highlights the influences that Toledo had on Tatum and, likewise, the influence that Tatum had on Toledo, placing Tatum's rise to fame in New York City into perspective. Also, the lack of emphasis on Tatum's early years in Toledo by other scholars has caused errors in the accurate documenting of Tatum's biography. One such error is the recording of Tatum's birthdate. Yet another inaccuracy, discussed in following chapters, is the influence of individuals and families, such as the Stewarts, on Tatum's career.

Community plays a key role in the life of all children. Tatum's unique talents did not make him an exception. On the contrary, jazz, commonly called 'the working man's music,' evolved from the community of African Americans. The popularity of jazz created an artificial relationship between blacks and whites. Tatum

---

[121] James Lester, Too Marvelous for Words (Oxford University Press: New York, 1994) 31.

was part of the community that founded this art form and this synthesis of white and black entertainment. Tatum's family and neighbors' and friends' perceptions of his family make significant contributions to the knowledge of Tatum. Biographer Lester's comment about Tatum's drinking is another reason why a study of Tatum in Toledo is important. He writes:

Mrs. Allen recalls that it was common knowledge in the neighborhood that in Art's adolescence and early adulthood he was devoted to drinking bootleg beer, and the fact that this doesn't seem to have caused any family problems seems mysterious to me. However, what I might as a white person, think about how a black family might have operated in this century, is surely based mainly on stereotypes.[122]

As Lester observes, a study of Tatum in the context of his family can help us better understand him. There seems to be no connection between him playing at home on his mother's piano as a child and his ascension into the hearts of his neighbors and fellow musicians as the greatest piano player that every lived.[123] Tatum's legendary image was a figment of the collective perceptions of his

---

[122] Lester 19. He goes on to say that "talking to Arlene I realized while the Tatums had high moral standards they were also flexible and realistic."

[123] Howlett 29. Likewise, Howlett writes that ". . . no one seemed to understand how he had developed into such a startling musician. Most people accepted what seemed evident: a black, almost totally blind child, son of a working family, was born with a phenomenal musical ability, an inexplicable innate talent."

public. To the extent that he was a performer, Tatum belonged to his public. He enjoyed a private world, however, that was comprised of parents, other family members, and friends.

CHAPTER TWO

Art Tatum, His Family and Neighbors

The purpose here is to gain insight into Tatum within the context of family relations during his Toledo years, helping to more fully understand the family's contribution to Tatum's musicianship. Because Toledo was Tatum's home for 22 years, the residents of Toledo would have been familiar with him and his family. Following are interviews from Tatum's family and neighbors.

Introduction

Art Tatum, Jr. was delivered on October 13, 1909 at 820 Mill Street by a mid-wife named C. H. Ferguson at 9 a.m.[1] According to Seymour Rothman, a <u>Blade</u> reporter, Art was born at 218 Mitchell

---

[1] Birth Certificate of Arthur Tatum Jr. - State of Ohio, Bureau of Vital Statistics, Columbus.

Street in Toledo.[2] This home, according to Arlene, was the family's first home and actual site of Art's birth. The family later moved, when Tatum was still a child, to the four-bedroom house at 1123 City Park in the Pinewood District of Toledo where Arlene, Tatum's youngest sister, resides today. Art was the oldest of three children. Carl, eleven years younger than Art, was a successful athlete at Scott High School from 1935 to 1937.[3] Arlene Tatum was nine years younger than Tatum. There was also a brother born before Tatum who died shortly after birth.[4] The family seemed typical of northern middle-class African American families. Arlene also recalls her paternal grandmother as being a member of the household.

Growing Up in the Tatum Family
Tatum's Early Problems with Vision

Tatum was a child with a special problem. He was born with cataracts in both eyes, and he could see only in black and white.[5] According to Seymour Rothman, "when Tatum was 3 years old he

---

[2] Rothman, "Art Tatum's Toledo Years" 12. This is the address that Rothman used in his article, "Art Tatum's Toledo Years." According to Tatum's birth certificate, the birth took place on Mill Street.
[3] As confirmed by elementary school pictures.
[4] Arlene Taylor, personal interview, March 1992.
[5] Doerschuk 22.

contracted diphtheria, measles, and scarlet fever. The diseases left him blind. He underwent a series of operations, and by age eleven could see things held close in front of him."[6] The series of operations, which totaled thirteen, restored vision to one eye. His restored vision, however, did not last long. As a young man, Tatum, on his way home from an after-hours club, an assailant with a blackjack was assaulted Tatum,[7] leaving him with twenty-five percent vision in one eye and complete blindness in the other.[8] The operations to save Tatum's eyes after the assault were performed at Flower Hospital in Toledo. B. F. Adamses, a neighbor, told the story of his assault to Blade Reporter, Rothman:

It was night in his early Toledo period when Tatum lost what little eyesight he had gained through the painful series of childhood operations. After a session at the Chateau, friends would drop Tatum off at City Park and Dorr Street. He enjoyed walking the short, familiar block to his house in the cool of the morning. Art whistled with the same trueness of note that he played piano, and people along the way grew to recognize this early morning song as coming from their brilliant young neighbor-pianist. This brought [Mr. Adamses] to the door in a rush, in time to see the blind pianist

---

[6] Rothman, "The Art of Tatum," 12.
[7] Doerschuk 22.
[8] Doerschuk 22.

struggling with an assailant who had blackjacked him. As he [Mr. Adamses] raced down the stairs of his home, the assailant broke away and fled. Art was helped into the house. The blackjack had caught him in the eye. Dr. B. E. Leatherman came immediately and administered emergency treatment. The next morning Art was taken to the hospital. The eye had been damaged beyond repair ...[9] Tatum had surgery and did have some sight return to his eyes. Light perception was restored and the first color that he could see was lavender which remained his favorite color.[10]

However, his blindness seems not to have been a hindrance. There are frequent stories recalling Tatum playing marbles, cards and football, as well as delivering newspapers. Writes Rothman, "eventually enough sight returned so that he [Tatum] could read for brief periods of time holding a book close to his eyes. He managed to play marbles and football with the boys. He enjoyed their company and they at least accepted his."[11]

Lester concludes that Tatum's need for people and his piano playing went hand-in-hand. Lester writes that he denied his blindness in ways that enhanced friendships.[12] Many of Tatum's contemporaries remember his handicap as having no real negative

[9] Rothman, "The Art of Tatum" 7.
[10] Rothman, "The Art of Tatum" 6.
[11] Rothman, "The Art of Tatum" 6.
[12] Lester 65.

effect on Tatum's personality. Billy Taylor, a scholar and jazz pianist, remembers that:

He [Tatum] was both strong and sensitive. He was blind and could hardly make his way around by himself. What freedom he did have, he guarded jealously. Though he was obviously limited by his handicap, he had a lot of fun. He loved to hang out and party. He was a handicapped person who resented, in many cases, the fact that it limited his mobility . . . But he didn't mope about. He was a relatively happy guy.[13]

Doerschuk saw his blindness as the source of his genius:

He [Tatum] loved his music and apparently enjoyed his life, but he may have been a jazz musician only in part by choice; to a certain extent, he had to love jazz, because that was the only outlet open to him. Tatum did have an affinity for the classics, but there was no room in the concert world then for a nearly blind black man.[14]

Although Doerschuk's comments correctly suggest that jazz was seen as having some kind of inferior status to the classics, that is not our concern here. The quotations are significant for their implications that Tatum's blindness dictated and shaped the direction of his talents.

---

[13] Doerschuk 21.
[14] Doerschuk 20.

Various adjectives have described problems that Tatum, since the age of three, had with his sight. These include near-blind, blind, and handicapped. Stories about his sight are problematic in that they vary from one biographer to another. This is unfortunate because his poor eyesight plays a crucial role in understanding Tatum from the years 1909-1932. The only literature based on an interview with Tatum regarding his blindness, "What A Blind Man Sees," was published in 1954.[15]

Tatum states in the interview that his sight has been the source of constant mistakes and curiosity. He describes his sight as follows:

While my eyesight has been more or less seriously impaired since I was a small boy--and while there was a period in my life when I lived in total darkness, I can now say gratefully that I have enough use of my eyes to attend football and basketball games and golf and racing matches. I go to the movies now and then . . . and if were it not for fear of straining what eyesight I have, I would read a great deal with the use of special glasses.[16]

Tatum describes the benefits of being blind. He believed that many sighted people did not appreciate the world around them

---

[15] Alfred Duckett, "What A Blind Man Sees," New York Age Defender 29 May 1954: Cl.
[16] Duckett C1.

as much as a blind person. He did consider himself handicapped but not unlike anyone else who might have to learn to adapt to a reading disability, or "psychological, or mental handicap."[17]

Family Life

Tatum's family were the first members of Grace Presbyterian Church on City Park at Woodland. In a church bulletin dated July 16, 1922, the Grand Opening Ceremony for the new church, Arthur Tatum was listed as elder and treasurer.[18]

Arthur Sr. seemed to have been the disciplinarian of the family. Rothman documents the family hierarchy as follows:

Even though the youngsters communicated mostly with their mother, Mr. Tatum's presence was always felt. He was the disciplinarian. He believed in the good and the dignified life. Father wasn't too happy about a paternity suit in which Art was involved in his earlier Toledo days, and it was fear of his displeasure that kept this sort of thing from happening more frequently. He believed in responsibility.[19]

Part of Tatum's upbringing included assuming

---

[17] Duckett C1.
[18] Grace Presbyterian Church Bulletin.
[19] Rothman, "The Art of Tatum" 9.

responsibilities. Among these responsibilities was the delivery of newspapers. Arlene recalls that:

My father worked for the National Supply . . . We never seemed to have financial difficulties. Mother worked out, and Art had a tremendous Sunday newspaper route so large, that on many mornings we all got up early to help so that he'd get to church on time.[20]

Art Tatum Sr. had a strong sense of family, and whatever property was in the household belonged to all of the immediate family. Although Art Jr. was the master pianist, Art Sr. made sure that the piano was family property and the entire family played on it.[21]

In an article in the Bronze Raven, Toledo's black newspaper, Grace Presbyterian Church announced that "Elder Arthur Tatum passed away Sunday morning at Riverside Hospital. An announcement was made to the congregation at the eleven o'clock worship service. The church offers its sympathy to the bereaved family."[22] He died after an illness following an industrial accident. His death came as a shock to the family who had always been quite happy together. Art was 43 years old at the time of his father's

[20] Seymour Rothman, "The Art of Tatum," Toledo Blade 14 June 1970: 6
[21] Rothman, "The Art of Tatum" 6.
[22] Bronze Raven 1 December 1952: 10

death.

Tatum's mother, Mildred, was born in Martinsville, West Virginia. She was a member of the missionary society at Grace Presbyterian Church.[23]

Tatum was born into a musical family, both of Tatum's parents were amateur musicians.[24] Tatum's brother Carl remembers that "My father played a little piano, a little ragtime, but nothing else. There was always music in the house, radio or the roller piano."[25] Arlene has mentioned in several interviews that her "mother played piano and a little violin;" however, Carl said she didn't play enough piano to teach Tatum much.[26] Like many African American homes, the Tatum home had a piano and a radio.

According to Arlene:

In a family where money was spent very conservatively, tuning the piano was an extravagance, but because it was so important to Art, my dad willingly paid the tuner to come out every other week or so . . . The piano, like everything else in his [dad's] mind, was family property, and we all played on it.[27]

Mildred was the first person to recognize young Arthur's talent. His

---

[23] "Obituary," Blade 14 July 1958: 15

[24] Doerschuk 22.

[25] Carl Tatum, interview on video, Art Tatum: The Art of Jazz Piano, developed Channel 4, WXTV, 1988.

[26] Lester 20.

[27] Rothman, "The Art of Tatum" 6.

mother played the piano and his father played the guitar.[28] This probably explains why Tatum, unlike many other famous pianists of his era and before, had the support of his family.[29] Although the source of his rare talent is unknown, Doerschuk writes:

> *Tatum also showed his talent early. At the age of three, he went with his mother to her choir practice. That night, while cooking dinner, she heard him at the piano, painstakingly picking out the melody of the hymn they had rehearsed. Soon young Art was learning his first jazz licks from the radio broadcasts and from piano rolls cut by James P. Johnson and Fats Waller. A quick study he exhibited near perfect recall; once he heard a song, he literally never forgot it.[30]*

His mother taught him what she knew about playing the piano. However, she also made sure that Tatum finished school before he began a full-time musical career. Doerschuk relates his

---

[28] Doerschuk 22.

[29] Ogen 112-113. Ogen writes that: "Jelly Roll Morton's grandmother disowned him when she found out he was playing piano in a New Orleans whorehouse. Eubie Blake's mother monitored his early playing and not the ragtime he could hear from brothels near his home and in funeral processions through the streets. Blake promised to eschew both brothels and funeral parades but by age fifteen he was working at Aggie Shelton's sportin' house." Lawrence Brown had to leave his father's house for playing jazz, and Willie "the Lion" Smith's mother told him when he played ragtime to stay away from the piano.

[30] Doerschuk 22.

mother's influence on his earliest years of instruction as follows:

After giving him some introductory lessons, she referred him to a local teacher for further keyboard instruction. For four years Tatum laid down the ground work of his massive technique, while polishing his Braille music reading at the Jefferson School For The Handicapped . . .[31]

Seymour Rothman writes that "by the time Art was nine he'd played in the church and made public appearances. His mother, however, discouraged these, as she wanted him to concentrate on going to school."[32] Mrs. Tatum's influence on her son was obvious.

The love that Mildred had for her son spilled over to Art's wife and friends. Rothman reports that "she [Mother Tatum] was close to both her daughters-in-law. She had a way of opening her home and arms to all."[33] Friends of the Tatums, including Russ Charles, a frequent visitor who lived down the street from the Tatum's, remember her culinary skills and the warm atmosphere that she had created.[34] Charles also remembers Mrs. Tatum as a stern but warm person and recalls Mr. Tatum as being a quiet but proud man whose pride showed in his walk. According to Charles,

---

[31] Doerschuk 22.
[32] Rothman, "The Art of Tatum" 6.
[33] Rothman, "The Art of Tatum" 6.
[34] Russ Charles, personal interview, 11 October 1993.

Arthur Sr. didn't walk bent over, he walked very erect.[35] Mildred died in July 1958 after the deaths of Tatum Sr. and Art.

Both Arthur Sr. and Mildred provided Art with different kinds of support that he needed early in childhood. Arlene recalls her mother's constant concern for Art. It would seem that early in his career Art looked to his mother for help in making business decisions. After Art's first European tour in 1938, he returned to Toledo. While in Toledo, Mae West called and asked him to come to Hollywood. Tatum sought the advice of his mother. She gave him her consent after she was sure that someone would be in California to help Tatum.[36] Although Tatum's success as a pianist helped ease some of Mrs. Tatum's worries, she never stopped being concerned about his lifestyle.[37] When Arlene was asked about her mother's death, she told Blade reporter Rothman that "I'm sure Art's death had something to do with it . . . When he died it emptied a lot of the world for her. For all of us".[38]

Other local Toledoans, like Casey Jones, a childhood friend of Carl, recount that Carl was responsible for Tatum's safe return to and from his musical engagements.[39] Additionally, other family

[35] Russ Charles, personal interview, 11 October 1993.
[36] Rothman, "The Art of Tatum" 9.
[37] Lester 5.
[38] Lester 10.
[39] See "An Interview with Casey Jones."

members, i.e., cousins, assumed responsibility for Art (See Harold Payne Interview). Eddie Barefield (a musician who lived across the street from Tatum and worked in Toledo during the early thirties) also recalled that it was a cousin named Chauncey Long who would drive Art's first Model A car which Tatum purchased when he first got the job at WSPD radio.[40]

Other members of Tatum's family could not be contacted for this study. Tatum had a son by Marnette Jackson, his girlfriend in 1933, named Orlando Tatum. Orlando was also called 'Booby.' Both Orlando and Marnette were accepted into the Tatum family, as were both of Tatum's wives.[41] Ruby Arnold, Tatum's first wife, was from Cleveland. They were married in 1935.[42] Tatum married Geraldine Williamson about a year before his death in 1956. In a 1991 interview with Lester, Carl noted that Orlando had died about a year or so ago. However, Arlene does not talk in her interviews with Lester or myself as if Orlando is dead.[43]

Also, according to an article in the New York Tribune, Tatum had a daughter, Mia Tatum, who was a singer. In the Baltimore area there was a son named Arthur Tatum Jr., who also performed. However, biographer Lester writes that Mia Tatum, alias Beverly

---

[40] Lester 53.
[41] Lester 82.
[42] Lester 92.
[43] Lester 231n5.

White or Magnolia White, born in 1910 and died in 1988 or 1989, was too old to be fathered by Tatum. According to Lester, she took the name to increase her popularity. Although she had talent, she died "in obscurity and in poverty."[44] Likewise, Arthur Tatum Jr. adopted the name to increase the success of his career in the Baltimore, Maryland area and he is also presumed dead and an impostor.[45] At the time of this writing all of Tatum's alleged children, including Orlando, whose paternity has been established, are reported by Lester as dead.

Art Tatum's Relationship with His Siblings

A Discussion of Carl Tatum

The videotaped oral interview of Tatum's brother--"Art Tatum: The Art of Jazz Piano," produced and directed at Channel 4 in Cleveland, Ohio (1988)--and this study's oral taped interview of Tatum's sister Arlene (who resides in Toledo) are the only primary materials from the Tatum family.[46] Carl and Arlene are the two immediate living relatives to Tatum. In addition to his brother and

---

[44] Lester 192-197.
[45] Lester 187-92.
[46] Howard Johnson, "Art Tatum: The Art of Jazz Piano," directed and produced by Howard Johnson, 1988.

sister, also surviving Art are his wife, Geraldine (presently residing in California) and a niece, Lucille B. Johnson--Arlene's daughter--who also lives in Toledo with her family.[47] While other scholars such as Felicity Howlett in her dissertation have been able to contact Carl Tatum, his direct input has not been found in any other oral or written interviews to date. We can only conclude that Carl Tatum has decided to leave Tatum's family legacy to their sister. However, a sense of Carl's relationship with Art can be discerned from these few sources.

Carl was the youngest of the three children. The following is how he remembered Art in his childhood.

When we were in Toledo, Ohio I imagine I was about four or five years old at the time and I couldn't relate exactly as to what he was doing, but then as I grew older I understood what he was doing. Of course, he was much older than I am, and I realize because I would hear him playing, he and his friends would come in and they would be playing the piano and then I realized that he was going to be a talent. My father is from North Carolina, but they came here at a young age. My father played a little piano, a little ragtime, but nothing basic. There was always

---

[47] Geraldine Tatum, letter to Dr. Roger Ray, 1992. Roger Ray Files *The Genius of Tatum: Toledo Celebrates Tatum*, University of Toledo, Toledo. Her address was still in Los Angeles, California.

music in the house, radio or the roller piano.[48]

According to the other people who were interviewed, Carl was responsible for Art's arrival at various playing jobs. Casey Jones remembers Carl taking Tatum back and forth to different clubs in the city. Carl, however, achieved his own fame in Toledo. As reported by Casey Jones, he apparently was quite an athlete.[49] Carl went to Benedict College in South Carolina. After graduation from college, Carl played basketball for the Harlem Globetrotters until he hurt his back. After his injury, Carl traveled with Art for several years before he married. Carl remembers that "the biggest thing about traveling with Art was being with him. I was proud being introduced as 'Art's brother' because so many people loved him . . ."[50] In fact, according to recently discovered letters from Bert Hicks (Adelaide Hall's husband) in the personal papers of Ella P. Stewart (the wife of Tatum's agent William Stewart), Carl was sent to be with his brother in 1932 when Tatum left Toledo to tour with Adelaide Hall.[51] Carl remembers that:

He started getting work in the clubs and followed Teddy Wilson. Teddy Wilson was the house pianist in band for Lou Reiner

---

[48] Howard Johnson, "Art Tatum: The Art of Jazz Piano," directed and produced by Howard Johnson, 1988.
[49] See "An Interview with Casey Jones."
[50] Rothman, "The Art of Tatum" 9.
[51] Art Tatum files, Toledo Public Library Files located in Local History Department.

and then Teddy left and then Art took over his position. Toledo was one of the most unusual cities at that time. There was no racial conflict, never has been in Toledo. That was unusual, at the time. He played there for about five years, four to five years and then got this opportunity with Adelaide.[52] It was a great thrill for the family to know that he was working with Adelaide Hall.[53] She responded to him and he responded to her and I think they had a good relationship, which was going to be terminated eventually due to his popularity and things like that, but they had a good relationship. He spoke well of Adelaide and the opportunity she gave him to be known and to perform.[54] It became evident that he was to be

---

[52] Rothman, "The Art of Tatum" 7. Adelaide Hall who became famous in the Cotton Revue took Tatum out of Toledo, writes Rothman.

[53] Ella P. Stewart, interview, Afro Americans in Toledo, Ohio. Toledo Public Library, Toledo. In Stewart's interview she retells the story of Adelaide Hall's needing a piano player to replace her pianist who was ill. Adelaide was staying with the Dr. and E.P. Stewart in rooms above their drugstore at the time. Hall liked Tatum's playing and he remained a part of her traveling show which went to New York. The Stewarts helped the Tatum family to write a contract (see Toledo Public Library Tatum files). However, the content of the interview reveals Stewart's discontent with Art Tatum Jr.'s attitude from his Toledo departure until his death. She recalls that he never came by to see her when he was in town or came to her and her husband's hotel when they were in New York. She seemed to feel that he owed her. The letter was addressed to her from Adelaide's husband. Throughout this research there is a sense of a "canonizing impulse at work in the stories" of Art Tatum. However, in the search for a fuller understanding of Tatum, Stewart's interview was most helpful.

[54] Laubich and Spencer x. "Art Tatum made his first official recording performance on August 5, 1932. He appeared with a small ensemble accompanying the singer Adelaide Hall."

famous.[55]

Although Tatum was very independent, it seems that the responsibility for Tatum shifted between Carl and Arlene.[56]

Sometimes the responsibility involved other members of the family, outside of those who lived in Toledo. When Tatum went to Hollywood in 1938, there was a cousin who lived on the west coast who took care of him. Arlene did not travel with Tatum, but went to Hollywood later to take care of him. The two younger children's recollections of Tatum's priority in the family were sometimes focused on either the money spent for his lessons, as Carl recalls, or, according to Arlene, on their mother's concern for Tatum's well-being. Carl said that:

He [Art Sr.] spent a small fortune sending him to a blind, handicapped school in Columbus, Ohio[57] and he developed this talent as he progressed year by year. They fostered it to him. They saw he could do something. I image someone said "Hey, let him play the piano." The other teacher, Mr. Ramey, piano

---

[55] "Art Tatum: The Art of Jazz Piano" produced and directed in 1988 in Cleveland, Ohio at Channel 4.

[56] Rothman, "The Art of Tatum" 6. Rothman writes that "brother K[C]arl, 11 years younger than the famous pianist, and sister, Arlene, nine years younger, each spent several years traveling and otherwise taking care of their blind brother and were considered part of the "jazz" family.

[57] The Genius of Tatum: Toledo Celebrates Tatum program. (Toledo: University of Toledo, 1991). According to the timeline in this printed flyer/program, Tatum attended the school in Columbus and Toledo 1918-1920 (circa).

teacher who helped him with his initial basics, but after that he was on his own.[58]

Until the death of Arthur Sr. the Tatum household seemed sheltered, as well as happy and financially secure.[59] The family seemed to have been content in their community. Carl does not remember any prejudice in Toledo, whereas Harold Payne[60] remembers the painful years of racism in his interview. Also, Rothman, a **Blade** reporter, writes that "during his Toledo years Tatum stayed very close to the black community."[61] Perhaps Carl's relationship to the great pianist, his own popularity as an athlete, or their close family circle insulated him from the unpleasant experiences of racism. Another possibility is that he was responding to the camera and/or interviewer. But he concurs with these sentiments about racism again in an interview with Felicity Howlett and Francis Williams. Carl states that "Toledo was a little unique . . . Opportunities were there whether you were black, white, yellow, or green. If you wanted them, you'd get them somehow there."[62] Also, Carl's memories of his brother's early start in music in Toledo

---

[58] "Art Tatum: The Art of Jazz Piano."
[59] Rothman, "Art Tatum's Toledo Years" 12.
[60] Harold Payne Interview and Howlett 45.
[61] Rothman, "Art Tatum's Toledo Years" 12.
[62] Howlett 45. Carl Tatum discussion at his home with Francis Williams and Felicity Howlett, January 28, 1976.

are consistent with others that have been interviewed.

Carl now lives in St. Albany, New York where he settled after his marriage. He works for the Welfare Department, teaches health education in the evening, and coaches basketball at PS 68 Community Center in Harlem in season.[63]

In an interview taken from a videotape entitled <u>The Art of Jazz Piano</u>,[64] Carl discusses Tatum's music and his reactions to his brother and his music. Carl concludes that:

> They mixed the stride and rag and then he had the ability that other pianists just didn't have their mind.[65] He could do things very quickly with his mind and his brain. He could improvise and he could do things that they just couldn't do, no way they could do it because they weren't him. Do you know what I mean--they just weren't Art Tatum and that's the way the cookie goes--they weren't him.

> If [anybody thinks] a musician has it easy then they are just kidding themselves. It is kind of unhealthy because you are

---

[63] Rothman, "The Art of Tatum" 9. This is still the most current information to date on Carl Tatum.

[64] "Art Tatum: The Art of Jazz Piano," videotape produced and directed in 1988 in Cleveland, Ohio at Channel 4.

[65] Laubich and Spencer vii. Laubich's forward written by Felicity Howlett confirms that "Tatum is the most articulate representative of the tradition formed from the merging of ragtime, Dixieland and blues piano into stride and from there into and through the piano developments of the swing era.

doing a Tuesday to a Saturday or Sunday booking and then you have to leave out of there and go to the next booking and you are riding planes, basically that's your mode of transportation, the plane. You have to go in bad weather and good weather. He would stay out practically all night. That's just part of him.

Interview of Arlene Tatum Taylor

Introduction

Arlene Taylor was born nine years after Tatum.[66] She still lives in the family home where Tatum spent most of his childhood years. She and the author continue to correspond. Plans have been made to visit Carl in New York. Arlene's willingness to communicate is another reason why she is considered the family's spokesperson. Also, at the successful tribute to Art Tatum, Arlene was the only member of the Tatum family present during the celebration. Roger Ray, coordinator of the event, said that he was unable to reach Carl or Orlando for the tribute.[67] Included within the celebration's files was a memo with the phone number of Geraldine Williamson

---

[66] Lester 16. Arlene's birth certificate could not be found in the Toledo Bureau of Vital Statistics. When asked about her age; she failed to answer.
[67] Roger Ray, personal interview, 11 April 1992.

Tatum.

Arlene was interviewed in the family home on March 24, 1992. She was interviewed in the evening shortly after having arrived home from her job as an in-home care provider for the elderly. I had met Arlene at the *The Genius of Jazz: Toledo Celebrates Tatum* and she consented to be interviewed. I sat in the living room on the couch and she sat in an overstuffed rocking chair with her feet on an ottoman across from a floor-model television set. She later told me that her family was one of the first black families to own a television. Surrounding us were the relics of Mildred's and Arlene's interior decorating. Unless asked, it was impossible to discern which memorabilia were Mildred's and which belonged to Arlene. For instance, I inquired about a photograph, an award, or the location of the family piano--which previously was adjacent to the front entrance, along the wall, near the steps. This space is presently occupied by other family keepsakes. Not far away is a child's rocking chair. Seated in the rocking chair is a worn, dusty, stuffed animal (Art's Teddy Bear?). One gets the feeling that during Arlene's interview, when she describes Tatum's favorite Teddy bear, that this could be the same one. In this atmosphere, it was easy to be carried back to the early 1900s and Tatum's childhood.

Arlene's description of his childhood varies little from earlier writings. In fact, she still leaves the question of his birthdate open to interpretation, indicating that he was born in 1910 but someone has changed the date on the birth certificate to 1909.[68] Howlett writes that:

> biographical information is in such an elementary state that Tatum's birthdate has rarely appeared in print correctly. One promotional article created for radio broadcast in connection with a release of a Capital Records album of Tatum solos in 1949 contains the correct date. (Would Tatum have had any reason for deliberately concealing the date of his birth?) While doing biographical research on the West Coast, Steve Ettinger checked Tatum's birth certificate and found that he was born on October 1909 rather than as commonly assumed in 1910. Thus, he has corrected an error that was virtually accepted as general knowledge.[69]

The interview with Arlene did not answer Howlett's other question regarding Tatum's need to change his birthdate or why it was changed. One could only guess that Tatum, in order to gain entry to and perform in saloons and after-hours, had to misrepresent his age. Bob Doerschuk, <u>Keyboard Magazine</u> writer, records Tatum playing his first gig with a dance band at 16, working the local circuit--The Rotary Club, the Toledo Club, etc. Howlett also

---

[68] See birth certificate.
[69] Howlett 9.

writes that "early performance opportunities that Tatum and his friends found may not have been those selected by their parents, but they were highly satisfactory for the young performers."[70]

Arlene's interview does reveal more about the personalities of their parents. She also substantiates earlier interviews with Seymour Rothman, Blade reporter, about her father being the disciplinarian, usually quiet and in the background, while her mother was the person who was around them more.[71] Mildred taught them many of the values that they later exhibited in life, such as Tatum's ability to work and provide for himself.[72] However, Mildred also did some correcting of her children's behavior, as Arlene reveals in her story about the first time she [Arlene] disobediently cut her hair. Tatum played the piano for long hours in Toledo's after-hours. Through Arlene's interview we begin to understand Tatum's discipline when we understand his parents and their influence on his childhood. Arlene's interview is the inside story of Tatum's family life and reveals an intimate look at his home environment.

After Arlene's explanation of Orlando's birth, his army career, and current residence in Spain, she showed me Orlando's picture. She explains that Orlando is Tatum's only son, although

---

[70] Doerschuk 45.
[71] Rothman, "The Art of Tatum" 9.
[72] Rothman, "The Art of Tatum" 10.

there have been rumors about other children. Tatum was sued for the care of Orlando when he came home to visit in 1947.[73] Marnette Jackson Collins apparently sued Tatum for $3,735. The article goes on to say that in 1933 Tatum had agreed to pay $5 a week to Marnette for his then 14-year old son. Tatum had only paid $14 of the agreed upon amount. Marnette wanted to seize Tatum's car. This, however, is not addressed in Arlene's interview.

Although Arlene seems to have stayed in touch with Orlando and consider Orlando and Tatum to have had a close relationship, this does not appear to be the case. There is still some confusion as to why she reports him to be alive and Carl reports him to be deceased. Lester agrees that the relationship between Orlando and Tatum was estranged.[74]

Across from Arlene on a table are photographs of her deceased husband, her daughter, and other family members. She sadly stated that she does not have much family left in Toledo. Her interview begins with Tatum's job at the Blade.[75]

---

[73] Toledo Times (July 25, 1947).
[74] Lester 82.
[75] There is no exact date when Tatum began or ended his job with the Blade.

Edited Tape Interview:

Arlene: Along about his younger days he delivered the Blade,[76] and we all helped him.[77] Later on he started playing places like the Rotary Club and so forth. Then he played for the Lasalle and Koch Company [a department store] every morning.[78]

Interviewer: Oh, that was WSPD [a local radio station]![79] How old was he then?

Arlene: I imagine he was in his twenties. He went to California with one of the movie actresses [Mae West]. She had a night club there and he started to work for her. He lived mostly in L.A. ever since, but of course, he would come home, but mostly he was in L.A. from the time he started playing for this lady's night

---

[76] Porter 22. Toledo Blade began circulation on December 19, 1835.

[77] Rothman, "Art Tatum's Toledo Years" 12. Rothman writes that "Art had one of the biggest Sunday paper routes in town. Exactly how the blind youngster handled his route is no more mysterious than many of his other accomplishments.

[78] Porter 79. Lasalle and Koch Company built a new store at the corner of Huron and Adams Streets in 1917, and in 1927 they added three more floors writes Porter. Tatum played the piano for the department store in the twenties for two or three years.

[79] Porter 79. According to Porter, Toledo's first commercial radio WTAL began in 1921 at the Nave Hotel. In 1928 George Storer brought the station and changed the call letters to WSPD. Likewise, the program for *The Genius of Jazz: Toledo Celebrates Tatum* states that Tatum was 17 when he was hired as a staff pianist by WSPD radio for a morning show (2).

club.[80]

Interviewer: How did he learn the piano?

Arlene: Well, we had a piano--we've always had a piano to my knowing.[81]

Interviewer: Where would it sit--over here? (pointing to a space by the staircase)

Arlene: Yes. My mother said that one day she was in the kitchen and she just heard this music and Mama said she came in and looked and Art was sitting there playing the piano. Kicking up underneath there, you know. She said she just sat there and looked at him. He was playing different church records and things and so then she went over to him and said what are you playing and he said, "I'm just playing different key notes." Mama said, "Well can you play so and so from church?" He said, "Yes, I'm gonna try and play it." Mama said he played it right on off. He had diphtheria and scarlet fever when he was young, well it left his eyes sort of bad, too, you

---

[80] Rothman, "The Art of Tatum" 9. Arlene is probably referring to Mae West who asked Tatum to come to Hollywood under her sponsorship in 1938. This was after his European tour and he was at home in Toledo with his mother.
[81] Rothman, "Art Tatum's Toledo Years" 12. Rothman writes that "until 1969, the piano on which Art started playing at age 3 and showed his real genius by 6 was still in the living room [of the family home at 1123 City Park Avenue]

know. I think that's what make the cataracts mostly on his eyes.[82] So they tell me that diphtheria was a bad disease for children at that point then. It would leave different things wrong with them.[83] But now it's not as bad, I guess? We have some things for protection.

So then, Mama said he just kept on. Everyday he would get at the piano. She said she watched him sometime and said he would be pulling up on the stool, getting to the piano and he would just play and play. Then she showed us the family aunts and different friends how Art played. He would just get up there and play. They would say well Art can you play so and so and so. He said, "I think so." He had a habit of saying "I think so." He played all different songs. Whatever they would ask him he would play them. Mama said it just got her because he hadn't been doing that, he was very small. I image he was around seven or eight years old and that's pretty young, you know. And so then his eyes got bad and he went to Flower Hospital and my mother had them operated on. They operated on his eyes and he told my mother he said, "the first color

---

[82] Doerschuk 20. Doerschuk does not document this the same as Arlene or Rothman. He writes that "Art the oldest of three children, was born with cataracts in both eyes." There is no record of Tatum being born blind. Arlene's story, of course, is her recollection of the stories that her mother and family told her. It is not clear what were Doerschuk's sources.

[83] Rothman "Art Tatum's Toledo Years" 12. Rothman reports that Tatum started to play the piano at age three and he also developed diphtheria, measles, and scarlet fever at age three. There is no indication to date which came first.

I see I'm gonna buy you that color dress." Which he saw was purple [or lavender]. When he got up a little to making his own money, he bought her a purple dress.

He was a pretty interesting character and I just run around after him. I was smaller than he was, but I ran around after him like he was some god or something, I guess. You see I didn't have but those two brothers. I had another brother but he had passed long before these other two. Art and Carl and I just began to grow up. I lost my other brother a long, long time before. My dad was born in Statesville, North Carolina and my mother was born in West Virginia.[84] They were married when they came here.

Arlene begins to talk about her father's mother (Arlene and Art's grandmother) and her presence in the Tatum household. Her grandmother lived with them but she did not play the piano. Arlene chats about her piano playing and her mother's. Arlene recalled the family's participation in church. She remembered going to church all day on Sundays. Arlene later joins Tatum in California in order to help his wife.

Arlene: At that time he was going to New York and different places playing and no one would be there with her and so I went to

---

[84] Rothman, "Art Tatum's Toledo Years" 12.

stay there. My daughter went with me when she was quite young.[85] She went to school here until he came home and begged her to come on down and go to school. She went down there and stayed down there, I imagine about a year and went to school there.

He died from uremia. He used to drink quite a bit of beer. He liked beer, but he didn't care too much for liquor, but he would drink beer. He drank an awful lot of milk as a little kid. We'd keep milk around there because he would drink a whole gallon of milk and wouldn't mean nothing for him for a day. He loved his milk. That's the reason it sort of surprised me about him getting uremia. Of course, I didn't know how it worked. I'm not medically inclined so I didn't know how it worked. That's the reason why we wondered about how in the world did he get this uremia so bad when he drink so much milk when milk is supposed to cut out a lot of things.

He called for me to come to California just before he died. I didn't make it; he died before I got there. I was going to leave the next morning and I didn't make it because my mother was here in Toledo and my husband and I were living in Milwaukee. At the time he was working there, and my mother said, "Art wants you on the phone, you call him and see what he wants." I said "Okay," and I

---

[85] Arlene's daughter was called several times during the course of this dissertation but she would not consent to be interviewed.

called him. He said, "Can you come here right away, you're not working or anything are you?" I said, "No. Sure, I'll come right away." Now I don't like planes, but this was one time I was going to ride one. Anyway, he died before I got out there. I was making arrangements to leave. He said, "Do you have enough money?" And I said "Yeah." My husband was pretty industrious you know and saved quite a bit of little money. Of course, we got that saving from my mother.

Interviewer: Who took care of Art's money?

Arlene: He did. Mama used to put his money in the bank. He would make different amounts of money at different places and she would be sure to put it in the bank. He had his little bank account.[86] Oh, a lot of people lost money.[87] Mama nearly kept everything they had in the bank. So many things happened long ago. But Art was pretty industrious and then Carl played basketball and Carl graduated from Scott, but I wanted to go to Libbey [High School]

---

[86] Rothman, "The Art of Tatum" 7. Rothman's article agrees with Arlene. He observed that [Art's] earnings were always turned over to his mother, who banked them in his name, and he made few moves without her advice and permission.

[87] John S. Rhinehart, "The Negro in a Congested Toledo Area," thesis, Bowling Green State University, 1940. Rhinehart states that during the depression years in Toledo, 683 blacks owned their own homes valued from $3,000 to $5,000. Percentagewise, 21.5 percent of blacks were homeowners, while 75.6 percent were renting and only 3 percent transient. Most of the 2,403 black families renting were paying approximately $25 a month."

so my dad went to the Board of Education and got some papers so that I could go to Libbey and I went.

Art went to Jefferson School downtown and from there he went to the Columbus School for the Blind after he graduated from Jefferson.[88] That's where the new library is now. It used to be the old Jefferson School there. It was mixed normal and physically impaired; the blind children went there.[89] I wouldn't go to school. Mama would take me to school and come back home and I would be sitting on the porch waiting for the door to open. I wanted to go to school with Art. That's what it was. So finally, I managed to make it through. I went to Jefferson and when Art graduated he went to Columbus to school. I came over here to Washington because we had just moved over here, and I had to go to Washington.

Interviewer: How old was Art when he went to Columbus?

Arlene: I can just about figure it out. I'm having someone put this [diploma] in a frame for me because you can sort of break it

---

[88] Wheaton 14. In 1880 the question of separate and segregated schools for Negroes in Toledo was ended. According to Wheaton the colored children were admitted to the Jefferson Street school along with the white children.
[89] Williams 39-42. Williams writes that "whatever the cause for Toledo's desegregation in 1871, Toledo was the only major city in Northern Ohio with integrated schools."

down there. That would be 24. Right?

Interviewer: Yes, June 13, 1924. This says Edna H. Ramey was his teacher and the Superintendent of Instructions was Charles S. Meek.

Arlene: I imagine he must have been about 18 to 19 when he went up to school in Columbus.

Interviewer: How long did he stay in Columbus for school?

Arlene: I imagine two years--a couple years. Before he went up there my mother had a white man named Mr. Ramey sign. My mother had him teach Art music because he was automatically playing since he was so good.[90] My mother figured it would be nice for him to know his notes and so forth. So she had them teach him notes. He knew his notes on the piano and then he had taken up Braille.[91] He taught me some of the Braille. I know what it looks like all right, but I wouldn't know anything about it now.

---

[90] Art Tatum file, Toledo-Lucas County Public Library, Toledo. According to this file in the Local History Department of the Toledo Public Library, Tatum studied two years at the Toledo School of Music with Overton G. Ramey. To date, no one has been able to locate Overton G. Ramey or any of his relatives for interview.

[91] Art Tatum file, Toledo-Lucas County Public Library, Toledo. According to this same file on Art Tatum at the Toledo Lucas County Public Library, Tatum studied at Cousino School for the Blind in Columbus, Ohio.

Arlene talked about her daughter, Lucille, and the family trip to Tatum's funeral in California, the family's relationship with Tatum's wives, and the reason why his body was not brought back to Toledo. She also described her childhood antics. We continued her interview regarding the location of the Stewart's pharmacy.

Arlene: Let me see, Mrs. Stewart's Pharmacy was on the corner. I think she was on the same corner when you lived around there. The drug store was on the corner of Collingwood. I think it was nicer then than it is now . . . All through here used to be the 'Gold Coast' and down at the corner where you lived you know and all down in here it was called the 'Gold Coast.' The people who lived down here, they were exclusive.

Arlene continued to discuss various people including musicians Rudolph and Mozart Perry's family,[92] and also the businesses in the neighborhood. She also remembered the relationship of the children to their elders. The following is a description of their neighborhood and her comparison of Art's, Carl's, and her childhood with that of today's children.

Arlene: I just think about how we used to go to church on Sunday, and sometimes like on Saturday we would sneak to the show or something like that, you know. But on Sundays was mostly

---

[92] See An Interview with Mozart Perry.

church day for our kids. We go maybe to this church for a while and then we go to that church with some of our friends for a while and then come back to our church. We thought church was really a good thing. It's something to think about.

I just noticed now white people lived all along here-- the Gold Coast. The man that run the shows down town he lived in the second house, his mother lived right next door to us. There was a white man who was a conductor, who used to drive the buses and street cars. They had the street car first and then they started buses. We were real little, and we used to come over there. And the white lady next door, whose son ran the shows used to tell us, "Call me 'Grandma Adams.'" And we would call her 'Grandma Adams.' Down here on the other side of Henry's used to be two white families. All of these houses were nice then, too, because people kept them up. They kept them up. It makes you feel sort of bad sometimes and you can't hardly walk a street now because you are afraid somebody is going to hurt you.

I think about what these kids are doing now and how we came up. How in the world did we change so fast? My daddy used to read the Bible to us. We got even Bible dictionaries here, you know, where different things happened. He would say "Look in your Bible and it will tell you why so and so and so is happening." He would even tell us "I hope I am not here in 1970, because I want you kids to watch out starting in 1970 its going to be terrible." He would tell us that, because he would read that in the Bible about these different things that were going to happen. And they are happening just like he used to tell us. Mothers and fathers, sisters and brothers were not gonna get along.

Arlene talked about the many awards, local and national, that Tatum had received. She explained her feelings about Toledo's indifference to Tatum. She also feels that on many occasions no provisions were made for her to attend these ceremonies. She continued to discuss Carl's absence from many of the Tatum celebrations and award presentations. She attributes his absence to a back injury sustained while playing basketball "a long, long, time ago." Tatum encouraged Orlando to play the piano by purchasing a piano for him when he was a child. She believes Orlando has the piano with him in Spain. She feels Orlando is a likable person. Then she continued to describe the childhood of her siblings and herself.

Arlene: You'd like him [Orlando]. He is a very nice fellow. The reason why I don't worry so bad is that my family does pretty good. They are not getting into something every time you turn around and that's the kind of family I like. Because you see, Mama would burst our head if we did something wrong. I didn't like them kind of families getting into something all the time, but now these people make you get into something.

There was only three of us coming up and we didn't fight a lot. The only thing they would do was get on me because if Art be over there playing marbles with boys and stuff, I'd be standing up there. Mama would say "Come home there's no girls over there. You don't need to see what Art's doing, he is right here where I can see him." Anywhere Art be, honey I'd be, looking out for him. Mama said, "One thing about [her] she sure looks out after that boy." Art knew it, he knew it. He would say--anything you want you get it. He called me on the phone you know, tell Mama "Let me speak to the baby" and I would go to the phone you know, "Hi, what you doing?" Everything he did, I wanted to know about.

When he was around Toledo, I'd be right behind him. You see, he would be down at the poolroom and I would get a couple girlfriends of mine--come on let's go down there and peek and see if Art is okay. There used to be a poolroom at Division and Indiana called the 400, maybe you heard of it a long time ago. That's where all of the guys went and played pool. Honey, we would go down there and go to the side door and peek in the side door until we saw Art. He used to take that boy there, the son of mine there [on the photo], he used to take him and put him in his buggy, put over here and Mama would watch him go across the street and then he would look up and down the street, because one eye was better than the other, look up and down the street and take that whole buggy and carry it across the street and do the same thing when he get to Collingwood. And the only thing he would have to do is go around the corner to Division there to the poolroom--over across from Third Baptist Church, it used to be over there. He would go to the poolroom and take Junior with him.[93] Honey, Junior would be in that buggy and he wouldn't let nobody bother him. "Hey man, you been drinking, keep your hands off of my nephew." That's the reason why I say those days were interesting days.

Arlene talked about the biographers and journalists who have been to their home looking for items, pictures, and information concerning Tatum. She remembered that his rocking chair, a teddy bear of Tatum's, and her mother's album are still in the attic; however, many of his things have been borrowed and never returned. She continued with her view of their family life:

Arlene: They come to me and get the home life and what Art used to do when he was little, what he didn't do, you know, so forth and so on. You get that from me, you don't get that from

---

[93] Wheaton 21. It would not seem to unusual for Arlene to be in the poolroom. According to Wheaton, the poolroom was one of the other places listed for colored women employed outside the home.

people in the street. Because I have heard an awful lot of fibs from out in the street. That's the reason I like to tell it just like it is. How we lived pretty decent lives. My daddy was a church man and my mom. I was whipped when I was supposed to be whipped and Art was bawled out, too if he did something wrong. Of course, me and Carl got whippings. Art hardly ever got whippings. We get together sometimes and just laugh about it now.

We were one of the first ones to have TV around here, you know when TV first come out. A lot of neighbors would come over and say, "Mrs. Tatum can we look at the TV?" and Mama would say "Yes." She was that way and then she would turn it on the station and say, "Now this is WSPD and this is so and so and so and so." She liked that, you know. People would come over and sit down, Poppa's friends come over, maybe some of Art and Carl's friends, they would come over. We didn't have a big one, just small one then when it first come out.[94]

They would come over here and look at the ball games. Art and Carl and my dad would sit here in the front room, honey, and let me tell you they watched some ball games as though they were

---

[94] Arlene is apparently referring to Tatum's trips home after 1932. Although television was invented in 1928, it was not widespread in American homes until the fifties.

there. You would hear them holler and laugh and go on. If there would be a big ball game on somewhere, Art would call Poppa up and say, "Poppa would you want to come to New York?" or "Would you want to come to Cleveland," "I'm in so and so and so and so, the double hitters gonna be," you know. Poppa would say "Yeah." "Well now, how you want to come? You want to come by plane or train or how do you want to come?" He would tell him which way he wanted to come and Art would have his chauffeur there to meet him. Poppa enjoyed himself when he was living because he loved basketball, football, baseball. You see my daddy used to be an ice skater.

He got hit, Kroger [grocery store] used to be out on Monroe, well there is a big building back there--National Supply--and my daddy worked there. He was foreman there, and a chain broke loose on one of those machines and hit him and made a place about as big as a dime and he died from that.[95]

My mama, she died right after Art. I think it was the way she said it. This lady was telling me she was there when my mother was telling her she would certainly like to bring Art's body home, you know, and she said she probably wouldn't have said it the way she

---

[95] Rothman, "The Art of Tatum" 9.

did if one of you all had been in the room where she was. But she said it was the way she said it. Mama looked like it sort of worried her.[96]

Related Interviews About Tatum's Family

Introduction

Many of the following interviews are from people who knew the Tatum family, but the largest portion of the interviews are contained in other sections. Together they act as primary documentation of the Tatum family and their life. They describe Tatum's relationships with family members. Their perceptions of the Tatum family help us to better understand Tatum in the context of his family. Many of the following informants confirm Tatum's love for his family and corroborate many of Carl's and Arlene's memories of Tatum. The Tatum household was often visited by the children's friends and seemed to be a place were neighborhood musicians would feel comfortable enough to stop in and either listen to Art Tatum Jr. play, or get help with their playing. Rose Newton, a friend of Arlene Tatum, also remembers that Tatum was very fond of his

---

[96] Lester 219. Lester agreed with other biographers about Geraldine Tatum's demands that the funeral of Tatum be in California, against the wishes of Art's mother who wanted him brought home to Toledo. The funeral was held at North Neighborhood Community Church in Los Angeles.

niece, Lucille. All of the informants recall that Tatum played an unusually good piano at an early age. Although Casey Jones wishes that he had paid closer attention to Art when we was running through the Tatum home, he remembers Tatum.

Interview of Casey Jones

Introduction

The interview of Casey Jones, a friend to Carl Tatum, is included in the following chapter. His insights add to the knowledge of Carl Tatum and the Tatum family. Because we do not have a recent interview of Carl, Jones's interview also acts to collaborate additional information we have on the family and provides us with a clearer picture of Tatum's relationship with his brother. He was interviewed in his home in April 1992. Jones's interview begins with a description of his relationship to Carl.

Edited Oral Taped Interview:

Casey: I think my relationship with Art came from being a friend to his brother Carl. I knew Carl Tatum and Carl and I sort of hung around together. As you probably know, Art had a vision kind of problem. I guess it was Carl's doing to carry him around to various places where he'd play. So, being a friend of Carl, I sometimes would just go with Carl. He would have to drop Art off to different places where he'd play. In that period of time we're talking about after-hour places where pianists played. Carl made sure that his brother got to these places, he would drop him off and pick him up later at night. So that's how I got to know Art. I lived at 650 Indiana and they lived on City Park, so it wasn't too far. I just lived almost across from the Indiana YMCA on Indiana, so it was a very simple matter to walk around the corner to City Park and over to the Tatum's home. I guess his sister is still living. I think they're in the same house. I don't know, it's been a long time to remember.

So that's how I got to know Art. You know, being young and not being a great lover of music, but I always thought he played tremendously. And one of the things I always thought was that he played by ear. I don't know whether he did or not, you know, I never asked. I just know he played extremely well and people enjoyed his playing and I enjoyed it. It wasn't something that turned me on, but now where it's becoming so that now I have begun to wonder if maybe I did miss something. I remember him playing and it sounded good, but I had no idea that he was going to end up being where we are today. Maybe I would have listened harder. I really believe now that I would have.

I think during that period while I was gone Art left the city, we both left. The thing that happened was that I went on to following my career as a basketball player and he pursued his as a musician. Then I lost track of his brother Carl and everything. I just remember during that period of time as I was growing up Carl and I were pretty good buddies.

Interviewer: Did Carl play sports?

Casey: That's exactly right. That's why I knew Carl and we got to be pretty good friends along that line. The Indiana Y is the place where we met and we both didn't live too far from there. I remember sometimes we would take his brother over to places where he had to play.

I was with Carl and that was one of the chores I guess Carl's mother gave him, or somebody gave him, to make sure that his brother got where he had to go to play. Of course, we didn't have automobiles, we walked, everybody walked during that time. That's why he needed somebody to walk with him.

Interviewer: Did he carry a cane or did he ever have a cane?

Casey: I don't remember a cane. I really don't remember a cane, he could have. I don't really believe that he did. The cane wasn't necessary for him to have. The thing that he needed to do, he could see some, now he wasn't totally blind, but if he had to go for a long walk or something two, three, four, five streets over and crossing streets and everything like that it wasn't a good thing to do. So they felt that his brother Carl should carry him to the place and then later that night at the end of the evening pick him up and bring him back home. These after-hour places went on all night. Sometimes it was the next morning when they would pick him up. They would go all night long during that period of time. They were known to stay up late.

Carl, I think would go home and go to bed and then get up. He usually knew about when most of those kinds of places break up and he'd go over there or lots of time other people would bring him back home. You know, when the party's over a lot of people did bring him back home because when it was over he didn't have to play. Especially on the weekends, most girls were just as happy, of course. I guess Toledo was known as the weekend town. So that's how I got to know Art, in a funny back door approach. Then when I would go by the house he was always playing at home. I guess you don't get to be good if you don't practice. You know for me, it was just routine to see him in there playing. It never bothered me one way of the other. I knew he could play and sometimes I had time enough to really enjoy him, but most times I was coming by looking for Carl and we had somewhere to go. You know, that's how it happened. I don't think I ever really got to enjoy the music like I should have. If he is one of the greats that everybody says he is and I have no doubts about that, I should have been sitting there awed, you know, going there to listen to him play, but it really never affected me that way so I think I missed something.

Interview of Rose Newton

Introduction

Rose Newton was interviewed in the living room of her home in the old Pinewood District on June 12, 1992. Rose, a friend of Arlene's, was only four years old when Tatum left for New York with Adelaide Hall in 1932. As with other interviewees, Rose's interpretation is accepted as her story of Art Tatum. Like the memories of other people interviewed, her story may have been colored by the recent publicity on Tatum in Toledo. I first met Newton at a local jazz club called 'Rusty's,' where a jazz session in tribute to Tatum was being held as part of the ongoing celebration. After many phone calls, we arranged to meet at her house, also located in the same renovated neighborhood of the old Pinewood District where Casey Jones lives. Also, like many of those interviewed, she was reluctant to be interviewed because of the amount of time that had elapsed and she was not certain of what she would recall. When the actual interview was conducted, her reluctance was replaced with many stories of her life in Toledo.

Because this study addresses Art Tatum, the man, and not just his music, Rose Newton's interview again gives us insight into his relationship with and image within the Toledo community. Other scholarship suggests that Tatum never returned to Toledo once he left in 1932. Tatum's return, however, was often noted by those in the community.[97] Newton says Tatum returned often because he was a 'Mama's boy.'

Newton, born January 6, 1928, is a self-proclaimed town gossip. She once wrote a gossip column for one of Toledo's black newspapers. She also admits to being inquisitive. How much of her story is important can only be determined by how the reader defines history. In an essay entitled "History and the Community" Paul Thompson concludes that oral history "gives back to the people who made and experienced history, through their own words, a central place.[98] Thompson, author of a text on oral history, contends that

---

[97] Mitch Woodbury, "Mitch Woodbury Reports," Toledo Blade 13 February 1947: 1. Woodbury writes that "Tatum has been back for a visit on one or two occasions, but he never has appeared professionally hereabouts... Tatum has been booked into the Latin Club for a week starting Monday evening."
[98] Thompson 37.

history is inseparable from its purpose. If one agrees with Thompson, then Newton's interview is important because the focus of this study is the examination of Tatum within his community. How others in Toledo felt about Tatum during his residency is significant. In this sense, Newton's interview is as accurate as any written clipping from a newspaper and as unbiased.

Taped Interview on June 12, 1992:

Rose: I was born on City Park. So all the while I was growing up I knew of Art Tatum. It was only after I got grown, it was in 1939 that we moved on Woodland and they lived on City Park facing Woodland. They always lived in the same house. When we moved in the 500 block of Woodland very few blacks were over there, in fact, we were the third ones.[99] They were always there . . . So, I grew up knowing of Art Tatum. Then when I moved over there, I have always been the nosy, curious one in my family. I knew everybody in the neighborhood and some of my sisters still don't know them. I would go around to people's house, especially where older people were, because I would always be around older people, you know much more around them. I would go around them and

---

[99] See Arlene Taylor Interview. She also says that there were few blacks when they moved into the neighborhood. However, there has not been an actual date established yet.

talk to them and his sister is a good friend of mine. In fact, every Friday it's a place we visit together, Art Tatum's sister and I. Arlene didn't understand, because of age gap, the interest I had in Art Tatum, but it was purely musical. I was never a musician. I always wanted to learn to play the piano, so when somebody plays the piano naturally I have an interest in them and I love music. Until this day I can't play the piano. Until this day I don't like what you call black music, "the buntabuntabunta." I don't like that, but I loved his type of music, the jazz and classical and the country music, that's me. So I used to sit and watch him and I was so in awe of him I didn't always speak directly with him, but he would be sitting there and I would be speaking around him. So, I made friends with his niece, Arlene's daughter and it gave me a chance to be around and listen to him. And the man was awesome. I mean, I have never in my life in all the watching of TV and listening to the radio, as I grew up it was radio, I have never, never, never heard anybody that I thought could touch his music. To me he was the music man where piano was concerned. I've listened to, well to me, he was to piano what this Marsalis is with a horn nowadays and I just admired him. The thing that interest me is my baby's godmother, Willa Williams, lived in the 500 block of Indiana all of her life. When she was growing up, she would tell me stories about Art playing out in the night clubs. You see I was too young to go, but she took care of Toledo's Mafia people.

You see, I was born in 1928. I was about six or seven years old when I started getting interested. He used to play down on City Park and sometimes he would bring his niece down there. He loved his niece. He only had that niece and a nephew and he would bring her down there and we would play with her. I was older than her, not a whole lot older, but I was older than her. Now back to 1930, I think he was about 26. He did leave the country. I don't think I remember when he left the country. It seems like to me I was just a little thing, but I do remember when he came back. Because during Joe Louis' heydays everytime those big shots would come to Toledo they would be looking for him. When I was a kid growing up, all of the big musicians, Hampton and all of them came to Toledo. Oh, did they [the Tatum family] dress.[100] He kept his mama in style. Whatever he made, he sent it home. I was just thinking about how his sister used to wear such big diamonds and things. Their father raised them real strict like. He was the kind that the man had to ask--the one she ended up with, was her second husband. Her first husband--she had to beg her father to let him in, literally beg. The only ones I remember real well are her and her brother, Art. Now

[100] Lester 161. Lester also documents Sylvia Syms, a popular night club singer in the 40s and Billy Holiday's reactions to Tatum's clothing and style.

she kept telling me that I should remember her other brother, but I don't. I said I never knew you had another brother. I know this one that she claimed but was he really her brother. But she kept saying "He was here all the time. I don't know why you don't remember him."

You know when growing up knowing something and hearing it all the time, it didn't strike me that here is a man unusual because I was too young to understand that. But the music, it was different from the commercials and things we heard on radio, but we didn't have TV then. You see, you all grew up with TV, so TV is your life. Well, we used to be tuned to the radio and it was only certain things that we could even put on. At that time we didn't know to be shame of "Amos and Andy." There was "Amos and Andy," "Jack Benny," "Rochester." There was music that came on with them. He would beat all that I heard. The only other time I heard music or something was when you stand across the street from where the night club was in the 500 block of Indiana you heard some music. They lived in the 1200 block. 1001 City Park [about two blocks away] is where I was born.

Well, he always kept people around him. But with his niece, it seemed like to me he just didn't trust nobody around his niece. He was real protective of them. You know, I want to tell you something.

Something else I found out late in life, all of this stuff you hear going on now with people messing with little kids, it was going on then but they didn't let it touch them--they didn't repeat that. If it happened to you, you didn't talk about it, so I guess they were protecting those kids because they didn't talk about it. He would bring her down there and he would stay down there. He didn't bring her and leave her, no, no, no.

Interview of Harold Payne

Introduction

Portions of Harold Payne's February 1992 interview have been selected for this section because Payne, a musician friend of Tatum, knew Tatum and his family. Although portions of the interview are also contained in Chapter IV "Art Tatum and Other Toledo Musicians," he also can contribute to our knowledge of Tatum's family.

Edited Oral Taped Interview:

Interviewer: Did Tatum read music?

Payne: No, he took Braille later. He said he might as well and I think his sister took Braille, you know, just in order to learn it .

. . I know she sent several people to come here and ask me for information, but you see she was too young to be around with him. You see, Art and I are about the same age, I mean if he were living.

Interviewer: Who was with him most of the time?

Payne: Oh yes, a couple of his cousins and so forth. [One was] Melvin Powell. I don't know whether he is still living or not. He had a little record shop over there near Stanley's Motel, but he had arthritis so bad I don't know whether he is still living or not. I'm gonna ask about him. Art had a lot of friends, though. I don't know why somebody tried to rob him. They claim that one eye got hurt and that's when he went pure blind. He could see a little, he could see enough to read cards. He would put them kind of close, but he had to know what they were.

Interviewer: Did Art Tatum date?

Payne: There was one girl named Marnette Jackson he went with. That was her maiden name.[101] She lived in the 800 block of Woodland. He had a baby by her, but he was supposed to have a wife in California, but I never met her. I never was around them with their private life and all. Most of the time I was with him picking up

---

[101] "Art Tatum Sued for Son's Care," Toledo Times, 25 June 1947.

and taking him up to a job and everything and bringing him back. I knew who his girlfriend was. Maybe this Taylor girl, I believe I've taken her home once, but he wasn't married to her too long. Of course his wife is in California. I never get it straight. I know there was a dispute about them but I couldn't verify that. They wondered why they didn't bring the body to Toledo to be buried and found out later that his wife in California didn't want it. When he was out in California he was well liked--that was Art Tatum. They just about closed up the whole of California for his funeral, and they wanted him buried there. Now his wife had the say.

Interviewer: What was his mother like?

Payne: She worked in private families, she was very nice. She never swelled her head about him. A lot of time you get to goofing off, maybe some Sunday morning. She worked in Ottawa Hills. Art come to the house and got me out of bed and wanted me to take him out to his mother's to get some more money. I said, "Where is it?" He said "I gotta be with you." He said, "Mom don't trust me with everybody. See?" I supposed she told him right. Now if I was with him she wouldn't care, it would be all right.

Interviewer: What about his dad, what was he like?

Payne: I never met him, I never did run into him. I didn't see his mother too much because she was working for a private family . . . He wasn't totally blind yet when I first met him, but after somebody tried--well I think his mother said that's how he lost his eye--somebody tried to rob him.

Interviewer: Did he change much after that?

Payne: No. I guess it kind of worried him, but see the wife he was married too when he passed away. I didn't know her. I never even seen her. I think they said they found him two weeks later in bed sick? I got the clipping of that, too--somewhere. So she must not have been, you see, like some of these girls--see money involved they do anything to make an easy life.

Interviewer: His first wife was from here, though, wasn't she?

Payne: Yeah, as far as I know. I think she is from here.

Interviewer: Was he living here in Toledo when his son was born?

Payne: I think so. Yeah, I know he was.

Interviewer: Was he excited about the birth of his son?

Payne: No, he was not. The only thing Art was excited about was a drink and a piano.

Interviewer: Did he enjoy himself?

Payne: Oh yeah, he enjoyed himself. You could tell when he got with Rochelle [a Toledo musician] and they got to playing whiz. Everybody got a kick watching them play, talking all that crazy talk.

Interview of Mozart Perry

Introduction

The bulk of Mozart Perry's interview appears in Chapter V.[102] He contributes to our knowledge of Tatum family life and helps us to understand the family in their Toledo neighborhood. Mozart, who lived down the street from the Tatums, also played the piano and was a young admirer of Tatum. He begins with a familiar story about a neighborhood pianist's relationship with the Tatum family.

---

[102] According to The Blade Mozart Perry died December 19, 2000, 8 years after this interview in 1992.

Edited Oral Taped Interview:

Mozart: I know one guy who was around Toledo, he is dead now, Herman Miller. They used to call him Herman Easley. He used to go down the street and wore dark glasses like Tatum and held his head aside working his fingers like this [he makes a popping motion] as he walked down the street. He could play pretty good piano, he could play the chord changes Tatum had, but he couldn't make the runs. He said it liked to run him crazy. I went to Tatum's house when I was a little kid and Herman would come up there. It would be 95 degrees and Art Tatum had just got off from work. It would be early in the morning and Herman would get up on the piano and Tatum would say "I don't feel like playing the piano now Herman. I've been out all night. It's too hot." I would say "Herman, let's go, the man's got to go bed and rest. Let's go. Call it a rain check."

I would go in Mrs. Tatum's house and play the piano, you know how kids are, we get up there and start playing. They all know me because I come around the house and his mother used to say "Arlene, who is that down on the piano?" She would say "That ain't nothing but Mozart. Let him go on and play. He's got to learn like the rest of them." I was about 13 or 14 years old. Herman used to come there, he was better than I was. She used to run him off the piano, but she would let me come in there and play it. That's when

I was learning, you know. She would say "Who is that in there playing that piano? That ain't nobody but Mozart." Those were the good old days.

She [Arlene] took piano lessons. I remember one-time Art Tatum was upstairs, and Arlene's mother had her playing her lessons. Art Tatum was there, he was half asleep and had one eye open and said "Mama she ain't playing that right. Go back over that. You ain't playing that right." He heard it way upstairs in his bed. His ears were so good he said, "I know that number and she ain't playing that lesson right." There won't be another Art Tatum.

Interviewer: What about Carl, did he play an instrument?

Mozart: Carl, no. He left here and went to New York and was a social worker, Carl Tatum, Art Tatum's brother. He went to Scott High School with me. Me and him are around the same age. He used to go and take care of Art Tatum's business until I don't know some way they got busted up and Art Tatum had a son from California that used to take care of his personal business, you know. Then he went on his own somewhere, Carl did. Carl lives in New York now. I haven't seen Carl in years.

Images of Tatum

Tatum emerges from the material of Chapter II as a bright and intelligent child. His ability to play "such good piano" is not the only reason, but his relationships with his parents and teachers also point to him as being a special child. With the exception of Art's vision, growing up for the Tatum children seemed normal for a middle class black family. Carl remembers that there was always music in the house and there were never any financial problems according to Arlene. Art's vision did not prevent him from having normal childhood responsibilities, like a Sunday paper route, attending church, and attending a traditional school. These kinds of discipline formed a foundation that Tatum later applied to his mastery of the piano and his career as a musician.

Tatum was a large-framed man. As a child, he seemed slightly taller than his classmates with a tendency to be stocky. His pronounced African features, full face, slightly closed and disfigured left eye, made him appear to be an intense young man. Photographs and the videotape "Art Tatum: The Jazz of Tatum" show him with a gentle and warm smile on his face.

In an active and lively household of three children and three adults, Tatum seemed to be the center of the family. Carl said that music became something that Art Jr. could do, and their father spent money to see that he had teachers to help him. This becomes the first of many times that Tatum demonstrates the ability to accept challenges that were given to him at an early age. Of course, a Sunday paper route was enough of a challenge with his vision problems, but the time that he had to spend at his regular studies, learning Braille, and with his music teachers must have required a great deal of patience and fortitude for such a young child. Many times he would stop playing with his playmates outside in order to practice his piano. His love of the instrument probably helped to turn this task into pleasure. Because he had such a phenomenal talent, the speed with which he mastered the piano is some indication of his ability to accept and conquer the other challenges that remain throughout his life.

In spite of Arlene's anxieties which prompted her to watch over Art closely, he would walk home some nights or early mornings from the corner of his block. He also went to the neighborhood pool halls. Tatum self-admittedly embraced the challenges that accompanied his poor vision. As Lester suggests, Tatum denied his blindness in ways that enhanced friendships. Other independent activities such as playing marbles, cards, football, and basketball must have taken a great deal of concentration for Tatum, but these activities probably provided him with companionship. Like his piano playing for social events, these probably became means not only for making money, but prevented him from being isolated and alone.

Tatum seemed very warm and generous to his family, not just monetarily, but emotionally as well. Arlene's affection for him was evident in her interview. He lovingly corrected Arlene when she played the piano (an indication of his desire for perfection on the piano). He also lovingly guarded his niece and nephew. He never seemed to distance himself from his family, even after becoming popular in New York and London. Newton recalls that Tatum came home often, and Arlene recounted several occasions when he called her to be with him outside of Toledo. Stories of his all-night playing at after-hours, his divorce from Ruby Arnold, and his distant relationship with Orlando, make one question his need for a family. It seems that everyone close to Tatum understood his priorities. He did what he loved, which was play the piano. The circumstances of his divorces are not clear. Tatum was a private man and he nor his wives has discussed their lives together.

Tatum's middle-class background helped him to afford the opportunities that enhanced his career. Carl remembered that his father spent "a small fortune" on teachers. As Newton suggests, Tatum's ability to afford nice clothing elevated them in the eyes of the community and helped to create for Tatum the public image of a well-dressed musician.

CHAPTER THREE

The Public Tatum, 1909-1932

Introduction

In Chapter II we discussed Tatum primarily within the context of family and neighborhood. In this chapter we will examine interviews of his peers, friends, and acquaintances within the larger Toledo community. This chapter is about the public Tatum. Although some of the people interviewed have aged and their memories have been clouded by the years and, additionally, their memories awakened by recent publicity on Tatum, their stories nonetheless shed light on the public Tatum and what it might have been like for him growing up in Toledo.

The author contends that their anecdotes are as valuable to the understanding of Tatum as are writings and interviews from his family. The focus of this research encompasses the perceptions of his family as well as those of friends, colleagues, and acquaintances, and what they felt and thought of Tatum, the man. Their interviews contribute to authenticating existing materials and rectifying continuing fallacies. For instance, many people have asked if Tatum was a recluse, if his blindness hindered him from involvement with everyday people, and who, in fact, were his associates? This chapter will help us to understand the image of Tatum that arose through writings and how this image developed.

There is much information regarding Tatum's love of people. Seymour Rothman writes that "Art's great capacity for friendship made him something special in the trade. Almost everyone who has discussed Tatum referred to him as "my friend" or "my good friend."[1] This image conveys the man's congeniality and his love of talk, both at and away from the piano. When asked what Tatum personally was like, Fredricka Scott Neeland, a Toledoan who worked and played original music of Tatum in the thirties, in a 1993 taped interview remarked that he was very quiet when he was not playing.[2] How we account for these inconsistencies can perhaps be explained by Joseph Campbell in The Power of Myth:

Myths are clues to the spiritual potentialities of human life... When a person becomes a model for other people's lives, he has moved into the sphere of being mythologized.[3]

---

[1] Rothman "The Art of Tatum" 10.
[2] Fredricka Scott Neeland, personal interview, 25 May 1993.
[3] Joseph Campbell, The Power of Myth (New York: Doubleday, 1988) 4, 10.

Tatum had not yet risen to international fame when he was in Toledo but later he was acclaimed by many as a virtuoso, if not a god. His friends in the community suggest that Tatum, as a child, was not special, that is, precocious. For instance, Francis Williams, a hometown friend, who grew up with Tatum remembers that "he [Tatum] was playing [piano] enough [at the age of twelve] to astound everyone who came into town. We accepted him as the pianist who lived on the corner of City Park and Woodland."[4]

It is later that Tatum takes on the legendary qualities that have been so often used to describe him. For instance, Jelly Roll Morton, an early stride pianist, upon observing Tatum enter a club commented, "Ladies and gentlemen, I play piano but god is in the house tonight."[5] Phil Moore, a pianist-arranger-composer, said "He [Tatum] had no secrets, no enemies, no hatred."[6] Not only did all people see him as their friend, as Seymour Rothman has suggested, but they saw Tatum as the model for all pianists, solo pianists in particular.

The following interviews from people who knew Tatum and were close to the musical world of Tatum during his years in Toledo will shed even more light on this interesting phenomenon. First, a

---

[4] Francis Williams, interview with Phil Schaap on WKCR, 3 November.
[5] A. B. Spellman, Jazz Giants (Virginia: Time Life Records) 6.
[6] Spellman 6.

review of Tatum's Toledo community will give us insight into Tatum and his peers' early surroundings.

Review of Art Tatum's Community in Toledo, Ohio

1909-1932

According to LeRoy T. Williams in <u>Black Toledo</u> "most black Toledoans continued to conduct their social and religious activities within a largely all black world" during the years 1915-1930.[7] These were the formative years for young Tatum. Although his sister Arlene and brother Carl have made reference to their schools being racially "mixed," the Tatum family had more social contact with the black community. Of course, two factors, his talent and his blindness, would make Tatum's experience distinct from other blacks in Toledo, as well as from that of his sister and brother. The following interviews shed light on Tatum within the black community and also the musical community which included white performers. During the twenties and thirties, black music was popular to both white and blacks. The majority of the nightclub owners were white.

It is important to try to ascertain what effect, if any, racial

---

[7] Williams 268.

politics and culture might have had on Tatum at the time of his birth through his departure from Toledo in 1932.

Following is commentary on the nature of the black struggle in Toledo?

During the earlier years of the twentieth century one of the major events that affected Toledo's black community was the newly arrived blacks from the South who had with consent been imported by the railroad industry as low-paid labor. Although Tatum, Sr. arrived in Toledo with his own money and was not a part of this group, these black migrants contributed to problems that began to develop among the blacks and whites in Toledo, according to Williams in his dissertation on Toledo's black community during the years 1890-1930.[8] Blacks, during the earlier years of the twentieth century, experienced economic and housing isolation from other

---

[8] Williams 183-187. Williams writes that "in the period 1915-1930 there were several responses to the growing numbers of blacks, as laborers, who entered the city in search of a new life. For prospective employers such as the New York and Penn Central Railroads (CLU) as well as the A. Bentley Construction Company, southern black laborers were vital to the city's economy. On the other hand, the city's Central Labor Union viewed the influx of a largely unskilled labor force as a threat to further unionization and a major cause of crime and delinquency." Williams documents the appeals from the CLU to the major to stop black importation into the city and the steps that Mayor Milroy took to help the CLU fight the railroad in this matter. At the same time the CLU told the city that the newly-constructed facilities on the University of Toledo campus for the "government training of men in the automotive work" was responsible for the city's shifting, workless element and the criminals as well (directly referencing southern black). Williams also documents a petition signed by Fremont, Ohio families to Major George Kinsey "to impose a ban on the importation of blacks.

groups (whites and foreign-born whites), leading to social separation as well. Home ownership for blacks was different in Tatum's time. Harold Payne remembers:

Our people are not used to apartments, you see people paying too much rent. But see you could rent a old ragged house somewhere around $15 to $20 a month. When the Brand Whitlock [a housing project in Toledo during these early years] was going on the rent was $20 or $25. They thought that was too much money, but it wasn't because it included their heat, light and gas. But, they didn't figure that in. They figured $10 and $12 a month was average house rent in the neighborhood. But when they got in the Brand Whitlocks they thought it was too high, but it wasn't. They started calling that Sugar Hill, the high-rent district. Turned around and found out how cheap the rent was they quit calling it Sugar Hill. Our folks had a rough time, didn't they. Sugar Hill, everybody going to Sugar Hill.[9]

Payne suggests how black housing separation from whites was viewed at first as a luxury and an indication of goodwill. Hope among blacks like this continued until after World War I. Although the years of World War I promised for some "the belief that black and white Ohioans had found in war and conflict, a mutual bond that would promote racial harmony and equality not only in the state but

---

[9] See Harold Payne Interview.

throughout the American society," this did not occur.[10]

In July of 1917, 105 black Toledoans enlisted to fight in the World War I.[11] In October of 1917 Reverend Henry Proctor of Atlanta, Georgia came to Toledo at the request of local black ministers to appeal to the city's officials to grant "more opportunities to the colored man."[12] Despite the unfair treatments of blacks in Toledo, the general cry of black citizens was to "honor the race" in the war effort. Toledo's black leadership, represented by Charles Cottril, "charged black soldiers to do their part in a warfare-based quest for equality."[13] Williams notes that some of the black Toledoans viewed the World War I in terms of the "crisis equals closeness" concept of human relations.[14] According to this concept the crisis situation of World War I and the participation of black soldiers provided an opportunity for improved race relations. However, as Williams documents, in Toledo the segregation and racial tensions of the past half century or more grew worse in the period after America's entrance into the First World War.[15]

Concurrently, black Toledoans in an effort to ease social and racial tensions chartered, established, and enlarged a number of

---

[10] Black attorney, B. Harrison Fisher.
[11] Blade 7 May 1917 and 3 December 1917: 5
[12] Williams 209.
[13] Williams 209.
[14] Williams 210.
[15] Williams 211.

organizations and religious institutions. Included in these groups were the N.A.A.C.P., the Colored Girls' Working Home, the Fredrick Douglas Community Association, as well as the historically active black churches.[16]

Williams documents other events that caused or showed periods of unrest for the black citizens of Toledo during the early years of the twentieth century. The three rallies, held by the N.A.A.C.P. between the years 1916 and 1917, were indicative of racial tensions. According to Williams, historically the rally, as a public forum, has served to inform, incite, and recruit followers to a cause of one sort or another.[17] Also, the Ku Klux Klan's public parades and speeches held in the city streets during the twenties were additional events that demonstrated the racial tension in both the white and black communities. The Ku Klux Klan's most active period in Toledo was during the years 1915 to 1944. Collectively, these were the experiences of the black community during the years of Tatum's childhood, adolescence, and young adult life.

Could Tatum be totally sheltered from these events? Could the young Tatum, whose sense of hearing and recall were so astute as to be labeled genius, not be aware of these troubled times in his own community? Was he always listening to sports and the music

---

[16] Williams 211.
[17] Williams 211.

of his mentors on radio? Did he not hear the news of the newspaper that he carried? How can one deny the intents of these Klan marches? However, there are very few of the following interviews which reveal any of these aspects of Tatum's life. Perhaps this is the nature of these more subtle forms of discrimination.[18] The racism that occurred within housing and among the labor and musicians unions are more subtle than the marches of the Klan. As Williams suggests, the black Toledo community did not experience the overt racism of riots that occurred across the nation in 1916[19] because of the institutionalized racism[20] that had been prevalent in Toledo since the 1890s.[21] According to Williams the black community in Toledo in 1916 had been held in check by a political system already

---

[18] Joe R. Feagin, Racial and Ethnic Relations, (Prentice Hall: New Jersey, 1989) 16. Feagin defines subtle discrimination as unequal and injurious treatment of members of subordinate racial and ethnic groups that is visible but not as blatant as the traditional door-slamming varieties of discrimination.

[19] Williams 199.

[20] Feagin 14. According to Feagin, institutional racism can be illustrated by societal practices that lead to large numbers of black children suffering and many times this form of racism reflects simply a desire to protects one's own social and economic privileges.

[21] Williams 199-206. Williams writes that "certain aspects of "law enforcement" in the city precluded racial violence. From 1917 through the early 1920s Toledo resembled a modified "vigilante community" with citizens, both authorized and unauthorized participating in "efforts to uphold the law." One could argue that in times like these blacks in Toledo were controlled by the institution that made the laws and the residue still remains in the memory of the those who were interviewed to stay in their place. Certainly, this would explain Carl Tatum's interview, which suggested that there was no racism in Toledo. This would seem true to him especially if he compared what happened in Toledo to other cities at this time that did experience racial violence.

institutionalized into the mainstream of Toledo's political and social life.

Oral Taped Interviews

Introduction

The following interviews will begin with an introduction, followed by the edited taped interview. The interviews will be followed with an analysis of their importance to the understanding of Tatum during the years 1909-1932.

Although many aspects of Toledo's black life cannot be ascertained from these interviews, much can be derived from the informants' impressions of Tatum within the Toledo community. They speak of his personality and the legend comprising the image of Tatum, and they create for us a sense of the community from which he emerged.

Interview of Casey Jones

Introduction

Casey Jones was a friend of Tatum's brother, Carl, and a frequent visitor in the Tatum house. Casey's wife, Lovell, who is not interviewed on the taped interview, also lived down the street from

Tatum on Mill Street when she was a child.[22] Because she was very young at the time and did not remember Art that well, she did not want to be interviewed. Casey Jones is also one of Toledo's black political leaders and currently resides in a newly restored section of the old Pinewood District near downtown Toledo.[23]

Casey exhibited some sense of written history. As an Ohio State Representative in 1975, Casey "was one of the prime sponsors of House Bill 87, which requires that history, geography, and government taught in schools include the study of minority groups," according to a paid advertisement appearing in an undated issue of the Toledo Journal, Toledo's only black-owned newspaper.[24]

Although Casey admitted in his interview that because of his association with Carl, he should have been more familiar with Tatum's music. He also seemed to lack a sense of the black struggle or what Tamara Hareven calls "a sense of its history." His knowledge of Tatum's history within the community (generational memory)[25]

---

[22] Arlene Taylor, personal interview, 5 April 1992. Arlene mentions Lovell, Casey's wife, in her interview.

[23] Casey Jones, resume. State Representative, House District 45, Lucas County, Ohio (concluding eleventh term).

[24] Toledo Journal, paid political advertisement. Undated. Jones was also responsible for black history curriculum being voted into Ohio legislation and the Martin Luther King Holiday Bill that made Ohio one of the first states to recognize this holiday.

[25] Tamara Hareven, "The Search for Generational Memory," Oral History, ed. Willa Baum and David K. Dunaway (Nashville: American Association for State and Local History, 1984) 248. Hareven defines generational memory as "memories which

seemed to lack a sense of history. This seemed strange from a politician who "was troubled with the way history was taught to me and my children." This comment was made by Casey Jones in the same paid Journal advertisement mentioned above. Instead Casey's views of history were the same stereotypical views held by the written history of the majority culture. For instance, he did not make an attempt to explain nor was there any evidence that he recognized that the occupations historically associated with blacks from the early years to the present were those of athletes or entertainers and how this might have affected him and Tatum. However, he does suggest in his interview that blame for the present problems among the youth in the black community falls on his generation's failure to do the job properly which is probably the source of trouble alluded to in his advertisement.

The main purpose within this section is to view Tatum through the eyes of his community. The generational memory demonstrated in Casey's interview speaks to the problems within the black community, rather than to incidents that are historically connected to and surrounding Tatum's life in Toledo. However, the problems within the black community and historically-significant events often overlap.

---

individuals have of their own families' history, as well as more general collective memories about the past."

This research also provides a sense of the collective heritage of Toledo's black community. However, Casey's interview seems to reinforce that collective perception of Tatum's larger-than-life image. Lois Nelson, a white Toledoan informant, perceived this collective memory to be a wall.[26] Nelson said, "You know my feelings about the whole thing is that there seems to be a wall, probably created by Art Tatum himself in his own community." Nelson, who easily moves socially between both the white and black community, refers to the Pinewood district where Tatum played as the "Bohemian section of Toledo."[27] Casey relates to the Pinewood district as his neighborhood. Clearly an etic (outsider's) view of culture, as in the case of Lois's observation, and an emic (insider's) view, as in the case of Casey's, will frequently differ.[28] It has often been the lack of the etic view which has been the catalyst for oral studies. For this study in particular, such has been true.[29]

---

[26] Lois Nelson, personal interview, 2 April 1992.

[27] Lois Nelson, personal interview, 2 April 1992. Nelson says that she could move between both communities, calling the section of town where Tatum played the "Bohemian." Also in a folder at the Toledo Lucas County Public Library there are notes written by an unidentified author. These notes also refer to Tatum playing at Charlies Chicken Shack and Waiters and Bellmans Club located in Toledo's Bohemian section.

[28] Molefi Kete Asante, The Afrocentric Idea (Philadelphia: Temple University Press, 1987) 141.

[29] Douglas Henry Daniels, "Oral History, Mask, and Protocol in the Jazz Community," Oral History Review 15 (Spring 1987) 162. Daniel concludes that:
> Although critics have written on these subjects, they are often
> outsiders more than they realize. While friendly, sometimes,

The following is an edited oral interview of Casey Jones in his home on April 17, 1992. He had just returned that morning from the state capitol building in Columbus, Ohio. His wife was present but she left us in their spacious living room and she continued with her housework in another room. She only entered the living room in reply to questions that Casey would ask her when his memory failed, which was not very often. Casey admits to a lack of interest in Tatum's music although he does refer to Tatum's popularity as a pianist. He probably captures the reality of the time: local folks saw Tatum as another talent and did not perceive him to be a legend until after he became famous. Casey was more attracted to Carl, whose affinity for sports matched Casey's, than to Art. He alludes to the presence of racism and how it helped provide an often "segregated" forum for Tatum's music.

Edited Taped Interview:

Casey: I always looked at him as a man and his music. I knew another person who played the same kind of way like Mozart

---

with the musicians, they are not necessarily successful in penetrating the color veil or the sense of protocol. Moreover, such critics are often ignorant of the nuances associated with American history and black culture, and the stratagems and ruses that Afro-American use when dealing with outsiders.

Perry.[30] Did you hear about Mozart? The two of them I kind of put in the same grouping and I knew both of them. The two of them made the rounds in the community, playing at parties. I guess now that you look at it, then we have to say Art was evidently much better, but he was older so therefore I'd say between the two of them I think Art probably topped Mozart because he was older. But they both made the tour around the city, constantly competing and if anybody wanted someone to play they had to get one of the two, they preferred Art I'm sure.[31] Because Art had been around longer and so that is how I got to know Art and I think I missed something now. You see, at the same time I started playing athletics. And then I completely got removed from the scene because as I played basketball you know I continued to play, played with the Globe

---

[30] Kathleen Stocking, Letters from the Leelanau: Essay of People and Place (Ann Arbor: The University of Michigan Press, 1990) 50. Stocking writes that "[Mozart] Perry says he grew up in Toledo in the 1920s when it was a little like Leelanau County... Perry says he got his name from an aunt who "played a little piano," and that he was influenced by Art Tatum, another Toledo jazz pianist.

[31] Bob Batz, "Stop all that jazz? Never, says 'Mo' Perry," Daily News Entertainment: 7 and 11B. Perry remembers that:

> "it was 1932 and Tatum was appearing at a little club on Toledo's south side... I was 12 and taking piano lessons. I'd heard a lot about Tatum because Toledo was his hometown, too. One night I sneaked into the club and sat at a back table. Although Perry does not refer to any competition between Tatum and himself, Tatum influenced the young Mozart. Batz writes that "by the time he was 15, Perry said, he was lying about his age and playing regularly for $1.50 a night in the little smoke filled clubs that dotted South Toledo in those days."

Trotters, played with all of those other teams, New York Komedy Kings. I played with all of those different teams across the country. Then I got away from here and I lost track of Art.

Interviewer: You mentioned house parties. Art made the tour of the parties, what was that?

Casey: At that period of time house parties were places where they would pour drinks and they would try to provide some kind of entertainment.

Interviewer: In different people's houses?

Casey: Yes, and most of the houses at that time had a piano.[32] That was the thing to do. That was the form of music they used in that period of time, just one person playing the piano.

It was something everybody seemed to do even if you went to church you didn't talk about you went to the after-hours. It wasn't the conversation that you have been to an after-hour--you wouldn't brag about it. Of course, the piano player always got paid. That was the kind of entertainment they had or just sometimes at birthday parties that they also played at. After being at the house parties where they served drinks and what not, sometimes birthday parties--Art played at birthday parties and things of that nature.

Casey: Sometimes the bands and things would come in and

---

[32] Friends of the Toledo Lucas County Public Library, 1993 Historic Calendar, "Daily Facts for August." On August 27, 1918 an "Orpheus" player piano cost $450.

Art would go up there and get the opportunity to play because he could really play and I didn't realize that, you know. I went to dances, too. He would get the opportunity to play with the lead band as they come in. You know, he didn't get paid for it, but it was an opportunity for him to learn.

Casey begins to describe the neighborhood, his main point was that it had been a safe neighborhood. He agrees with Arlene that the times were different. "Everyone looked out for everyone else." He also noticed that there are very few solo pianists, like Tatum, in Toledo anymore. Stanley Cowell and Art Edgerton are the only solo pianists that are interested in Tatum's kind of music. He feels technology is responsible. (By this he seems to have meant the rise in popularity of rock music and other modern forms of music which have created instant successes, through albums and tapes, without the dues musicians like Tatum experienced in earlier times.)

Interviewer: Could Tatum have heard classical composers and imitated or mixed his style with theirs?

Casey: Yes, his rhythm had that. He had his own style of rhythm. I guess he kind of reminds you of Louis Armstrong with his horn--a man with his horn. I remember him as a man and his music. You know, it didn't bother me one way or the other--like I said I wasn't a great music lover. I was so interested in sports I didn't have time to appreciate how really good the man was in his music, although I heard him probably more than a whole lot of folks just by the simple virtue of the fact that his brother and I were pretty good friends. Still, it didn't mean that much.

Casey: Art started playing in [the Pinewood District[33]], playing mostly to blacks. There were all kinds of after-hour places. Because this was a gangster's hang out nobody did anything to anybody. A drunk could walk the street and nobody would bother him or anything. It was a good town.

Another thing I guess happened was during that period of time a lot of people weren't working and had to do with some things, athletics, singing, dancing, those kinds of things. The Douglas Center[34] was the center and then after the Douglas Center went so

---

[33] Rinehart 26. Rinehart's thesis is about Avondale, Belmont, Fifteenth Street, and Indiana Avenue in the Pinewood District. Although he writes in 1940 many of his facts are taken from the years that are important for this study of Tatum's life and still remained true for his family during these latter years. Rinehart writes that:

> It is significant fact that 1,837 families and 1,252 single persons, or approximately 78% of the total number of Colored relief cases were allocated in the Pinewood district. Of Toledo's three Negro Communities, this the largest. It covers the sixth, seventh, eighth and ninth wards and houses 10,390 of Toledo's Negroes. The Toledo Beach Area on Toledo's East Side is the second largest Negro community. This community covers the eightieth, nineteenth, and twentieth wards and contains 1,043 citizens. In North Toledo the third community contains 1,040 citizens and is located in the first, third, and fourth wards. These figures seem to place Tatum and his family in the thick of the Toledo's black community (26).

[34] Williams 79 and 251. According to Williams, Albertus Brown, probably Toledo's first black attorney, organized the Fredrick Douglas Community Association [Center] in 1919 four years after he helped to form the N.A.A.C.P. in Toledo. "The Association

well, we came up with the Indiana YMCA.[35] So between the two of them we still had great places for people to go. The first Douglas Center I went to was located down there on 10th and Adams.

You know that was a period of time when people would just seem like everybody was welcome. It wasn't a problem that you didn't belong. Everybody just invited everybody else and nobody worried about anybody else. I think that was a time in history that has passed. Having been there, I say it was a good time, but then if you think about money and all of that kind of stuff, which there was none back then, today is a better time. Like I said, I remember during the depression when bread was five cents a loaf, but who had five cents. Now bread costs a dollar so you couldn't get a dollar, so you see the difference.

You know, we look at this and I think of Toledo history and I remember some things before the days of automobiles and most of

quickly became a center for the social and recreational life of the community," writes Williams. The Fredrick Douglas Recreational Center for Boys in 1919, "based largely on the concept of the white community's Young Men's Christian Association, opened its doors on Monroe near Erie Street... In 1921 it opened its doors to women and in 1925 the center purchased a building at Pinewood and Thirteenth."
[35] Lester 45. Steve Taylor, in an interview with Lester, remembers:
> When we were kids the Indiana Y was built on the corner of Elizabeth and Indiana--brick building right in the center of the 8th Ward, where all the black people lived, and in the lobby of the Y there was a beautiful grand piano. Now, Art used to come there--wasn't too far, he only lived about two blocks from the Y. So he used to come up there and play this piano, and people would just gather around....

the time horse and buggy and that kind of stuff and Toledo had harbors downtown. We had black trades way back at the turn of the century. Then as the city got bigger and bigger we started losing all of those things... [and] blacks had way back... They owned some of the hotels in downtown Toledo. Of course the bellboys, bellhops and all of those kinds of things were black. Our history shows that in this city.[36]

Interview of Gladys Herron and Jim Butler

Introduction

Gladys Herron and Jim Butler were interviewed at a neighborhood community center for the aged in Toledo's Pinewood District on June 12, 1992. Both of them remembered Tatum and his family. They can contribute to our knowledge of Tatum's early performances in the community and the community's image of Tatum, i.e., what was Tatum like away from the piano, did people like him, was he sociable, what was the extent of his handicap? They

---

[36] Williams 274-275. In 1890, the majority of "employed blacks, male and female, worked either as unclassified laborers or servants. These workers continued to hold primarily the same jobs in the decades of relatively small increases in the population (1890-1910) as well as in the years of accelerated growth after 1910. While the city's expanding industries offered some new opportunities, black residents remained largely concentrated in the menial categories of labor."

also can help us discern the effects of racism and its probable impact on Tatum as a musician.

Gladys Herron, a local hairdresser and business woman, founded the first school of cosmetology for the black woman in Toledo. She came to Toledo in 1925. At the time Tatum was 26 years old. Jim Butler, whom she invited in for the interview, is also a long-time resident of Toledo. He was the first black to work and own his own shoe repair shop in Tiedkes Department Store. Their interview highlights Toledo's black community life and lifestyle. While we are certainly interested in an inside report of Toledo history, our main concern here is Art Tatum. It seemed important to leave some of the stories of Toledo's black community intact, because very little reporting of the details concerning Toledo's black community they discussed, exists in traditional histories of Toledo. An example of this is the documentation of a black-owned business located on Dorr Street. However, some of Tatum's Toledo community has been documented in LeRoy T. Williams' study and many of their comments have been cross-referenced to verify the accuracy of their oral interview.

Herron and Butler's interview does not contradict any of the information previously mentioned in this study; on the contrary, it confirms the "character of Toledo's black community" and offers a sense of its flavor, including the prudency and Victorian modesty of its women. Imagine girls wearing skirts and blouses to play basketball! Unlike Casey, Butler and Herron frequented and knew Tatum on the jazz scenes, so theirs is a more intimate impression. They also suggest that finding gigs was sometimes a struggle because Tatum was limited by racial segregation to where he could play.

Edited Taped Interview:

Interviewer: When did you meet Art Tatum?

Gladys: Let's see. We were at the Douglas Center,[37] I can't remember when because we were still playing basketball when Clarence Thomas was the inspector down in records [official inspector although others were in charge of certain other duties].

Jim: I met Tatum around these corners shooting marbles.[38] The marble would be here and Art was over here and shoot and hit you, too. His eyes didn't focus. He didn't look directly at anything.

Interviewer: So he could see?

Jim: Well, he could see a little bit, yea.

---

[37] Toledo Blade. "Unlock the Piano." 27 January 1992. Peach Section: 1. Teeny Brown said that "we used to go there to play basketball, but when Art came in to practice on the piano, we had to quit. That was the rule there. They wanted it quiet when he played... Actually, they kept the piano locked all the time except when Art Tatum came in. Then they'd unlock it so he could sit down and play."
[38] Lester 25. According to Lester "family and friends have reported that he [Tatum] played a lot of marbles.

Gladys: He would hold his head like that and Art knew what everybody was doing.

Jim: Oh yea, he could see a little bit. He shot marbles. He didn't play too much basketball.

Gladys: That all depends.

Jim: Yea, he would come down and that's all he would play. He would get around and he was knowledgeable, but he didn't participate in any sports like the rest of us did. He was a nice guy to be around too.[39]

Interviewer: What do you mean, nice?

Jim: Well he was admirable, he was a congenial. I never saw him mad.

Gladys: I never did either. He had plenty girlfriends.[40]

Interviewer: Girlfriends? Now that's the first time I heard anybody say he had girlfriends.

Gladys: Well, he had them.

Jim: What you have to understand is back in the days we're talking about we were all together, didn't too many people get past

---

[39] Lester 25. "Russell McCowan, who was older than Art but who lived in his neighborhood, claimed that Art was able to play basketball largely by sound; he knew where the others were from the sound of their voices, and could even take respectable shots at the basket."

[40] Lester 81. Ellis Larkin said, "You know the piano player gets all the hottest chicks, the drummer gets the others, the bass player gets last... The first thing the women see, 'Oh, don't the piano player play beautifully.' And that's it! Doors open!"

Division Street and didn't too many people live in the 300 block, 400 block of Pinewood, maybe one or two families in the 500 block, but then you went to Woodland and there wasn't many. On Dorr Street there was nothing but us. See, we were all kind of in one area so everybody knew everybody, that's how that happened.

Gladys: I lived in the 400 block of Woodland, and everybody else lived in the 300 and 400 block. In fact, the few that lived on Pinewood and Woodland back to Vance [Street] and Nebraska [Street] and whatever was over there. We were all thrown into this one area.[41] You might have had a few people in Stickney and a few people in the north end and a few people on Curtis Street, but everything that went on went on in this area. So, that's why everybody knew everybody else.

Jim recalls that everyone was poor. He names Ella P. Stewart and Wes Gordon, a police officer, as the people who looked after black folk. He called them "influential... they looked out for the kids in the area." Jim said that prohibition:

began around here in the states that Roosevelt got in. Oh, you had your hoodlums and your wrong doers, but kids didn't know

---

[41] Porter 76. Porter writes that "the migration went on throughout the 1920s, creating crowded black neighborhoods in the segregated Northern cities. By 1930 residential segregation restricted Toledo's black residents to the southwestern part of the city, previously occupied by the Irish and the Germans." They are probably referring to the residue of these groups left in the neighborhood.

anything about it. Kids might have broke a window or rang your doorbell or something, that was the extent of it.

Jim: Art was just like any other normal kid as far as I am concerned. He socialized, he played and like I said, we all ran together.[42]

Gladys: Anytime there was a piano some place he would play.[43] He was as kind and as friendly as anybody. If we saw Art and we saw a piano we knew we were going to have some music.[44] After he left Toledo he didn't come back for a long time.

Jim: When he come back you don't know nothing about it, you wouldn't be in the club.[45] He always had his money in $5 bills on the inside of his coat, that way your money didn't get mixed up. Of course, Carl, his brother, was living then and he was

Gladys: I forgot about Carl.

Jim: Carl was his, after Art got big time Carl looked out for

---

[42] Lester 25. Lester writes that "... for his own part Art minimized his handicap and managed to have a nearly normal childhood. His teacher Mrs. Morrison summed it up: "He was as near normal as a kid could be and yet be blind. Bless his heart."

[43] Lester 28. Mrs. Morrison, Art's English and American history teacher from 1922 to 1924 recalls "every chance that kids got they took to the piano, and he [Tatum] took to the piano more than anybody.

[44] Lester 42. According to Lester "... as a teenager he [Tatum] was providing the music for social occasions--probably the one-steps, two-steps, cake-walks, and rags that were still so popular then... everyone wanted Art to play the piano so they could sing and dance.

[45] Lester 87. Lester documents that Tatum was "frequently in Toledo in the middle 'thirties... in 1935 he was Jon Hendricks's accompanist at the Waiters and Bellmans Club in Toledo.

him, they were brothers. Art loved him, he would buy him drinks fast as you want them--he had a heavy voice, always the same. He didn't like to play too much church music, though.

Gladys: If he played church music he would jazz it up because that was his style of playing. He was very, very good and you didn't have to beg him or anything to play. He played and he played beautifully and he got along with everybody beautiful.

Jim: Back in those days, Gladys, I think most of us got along. It wasn't like it is now. We were all crammed in there and the living standard was about the same for everybody.

... But Art was an all right guy. I don't know if anybody said a bad word about him.

Gladys: Never heard a bad word about him.

Jim: The nicest night club we had were Waiters and Bellmans Club at 535 or 545 Indiana. You could go in there, a group of ladies, you go in there and nobody is going to say anything to you, nobody is going to mess with you because Johnnie Crockett go get that pistol and...[46]

Gladys: Get you out of there.

Jim: If you were a lady when you went in, you were a lady

---

[46] Lester 87. Jon Hendricks, a well-known singer who lived five house from the Tatum's, said that "the Waiters and Bellmans Club was an after-hours, but it was also a regular club. It had a restaurant next door. It was a regular club during the day, you see it was the Waiters and Bellmans Club at night."

when you went out. It wasn't all this junk you going places and start fighting and tearing up places. Now that was the nicest one. Then you had the corner bar opened up.

Gladys: Oh yeah, but that was later.

Jim: Oh yeah, a long time later. You see, Johnnie Crockett operated the way he did because he was in with the Governor. They helped each other. That's how he could open that joint all night long. I saw the letter of his. That's how he could stay open all day and all evening. The white folks come out there too because they were going to treat it right. He could say he never closed. He was in with the governor.[47]

Jim: They had all those little knick knacks for 2-3 cents and we didn't have any money. But that was the only night club. You had some joints being legitimate places, but most of them were owned by white men. But Art, he started out at Chateau La France.

---

[47] Illman 89. Illman writes:

> Just as Toledo had a segregated district of bordellos long before the end of the 19th century, there were also numerous organized gambling houses, all protected by police. The word tenderloin was given by newspapers to those areas of a city from which police obtained graft enabling them to buy tenderloin steaks. Some of the most notorious establishments were Jean Ford's, Mother H, Three Aces (which featured black and white), Chicken Charley, Palm Gardens, Gypsy Joe's and Pappy's. Pearl Barber, a black pimp, was used by the police chief as bagman for collections in the vice circles."

These were places and events that Grace and possibly Jim were not allowed to frequent or talk about considering the strict up bring of black children at this time.

That's where he started in the big time. I guess didn't many hoodlums come in there.

Gladys: They saw what he had and I guess they promoted him.

Jim: That's how he made all of his money. This was the hoodlums haven here in Toledo. They would defend all of those racketeers from all over the country.[48]

Interviewer: So when Art wasn't playing at the Chateau La France where would he play?

Gladys: Well, he left town then.

Jim: He left town after that. He was just playing around wherever he could, at churches, down to the Center, the Frederick Douglas Community Center.

Gladys: But then as I remember now because when Art dropped his manager or what have you, did he go to Chicago or New York?

Jim: I think he went to New York.

Gladys: Then he was on big time, but during his childhood

---

[48] Illman 97. Writes Illman, "legitimate people feared moving to Toledo. Local officials claimed it was no worse than others." In a way they were right. Before Licavoli there were no organized gangs taking over distribution with hijacking or forced sales. Gangland killings or murders were virtually unknown. Local crime was under control." Toledo became known as "Chicago on Lake Erie" during the Prohibition era under Licavoli. Toledo was a known asylum for gangsters and mobsters to hide out.

he just played.

Jim: Just a regular kid, normal except for his eyes. He did things normal kids did.

Interviewer: Do you remember his parents?

Gladys: His mother and his sister I remember them because he would, okay the Wards lived on the corner across the street, Reverend Ward was at Grace Presbyterian Church, and Art would go over there and his family would be looking for him.

Interviewer: He would be at Grace Presbyterian Church?

Gladys: Yeah, he would go to Reverend Ward's and I don't know whether Reverend Ward would take him to church or church would be open. But I could remember they would be looking for him in the neighborhood and they would always find him over at Grace Presbyterian Church playing that piano back in that back room.[49] But his mother and sister...

Gladys: Yeah, she lives in the house on City Park. I know he had a sister and a mother and a father.

Jim: And a brother.

Gladys: Carl, but I never heard of them playing the piano other than there in the house banging on the thing. Okay, maybe

---

[49] Lester 19. Lester documents the home and the location of the church as well. He writes that "religion was important, and in 1919 Arthur Sr., and Mildred were charter members of the Grace Presbyterian Church, across the street from the house where the children were raised."

they did play, but they didn't play out. They weren't known as musicians other than Art.[50]

Jim: Art didn't get famous until he left Toledo.

Interviewer: When you heard Tatum could you recognize him, because you know you said he didn't get famous until he left here, but did he sound like an ordinary piano player or did you just know he was good?

Jim/Gladys: We didn't have records... He was just a player that we enjoyed his playing and we watched him play.

Interviewer: Did you dance, too?

Jim/Gladys: Oh, yes.

Jim: We'd dance, we didn't miss a step. I mean we could dance, we used to have good dances. I believe once a month...

Gladys: When we went to the dances Ella P. Stewart would have the girls sitting here and then she would see how many times you dance with John or how many times you dance with Sam and when 11:00 or was it 11:30 or 11:45 everybody went home.

Jim: We used to have a couple thousand people there. We

---

[50] Lester 10. Lester in his research has not found any documentation of either the father or the mother playing. He also mention an interview with Carl who said that he doesn't remember his mother [Mildred] playing the piano. Likewise all of Arlene's interviews including the one in this collection refers to the kinds of instruments that her parents played. I am inclined to agree with Lester that no matter what the case neither of them could have taught Art a great deal musically. However, it does seem important that Tatum was exposed to music at an early age.

had big time in our day.

Gladys: But the neighborhood people would recognize us and we were protected.

Interviewer: What was a typical day for you when you were young?

Jim: Going to school everyday. You didn't stay out. You went to church just like you went to school. 9 o'clock Sunday, 11:00, BYTU, youth church, at 6:00 and evening service. That was a typical day. In the summer time we would shoot marbles, we would play basketball. We would get on a bus and go play Detroit or go play Cleveland and went to Pittsburgh and Cleveland one day. We had nice, good, beautiful young people. We had pleasantries and even after we got grown I guess I must have went to dances all the time. Then we had the bigtime dances like the balls.

Jim and Gladys talked about entertainment other than jazz clubs in Toledo. Then Jim and Gladys described the stores in the neighborhood and the store that sold beer. Jim remembers that blacks and whites "were intermingled... A lot of white people lived on Avondale and Illinois. Mostly after Division, the right side of Division, four or five in the 400 block a lot of them lived there."[51]

---

[51] Lester 19. According to Lester "Toledo neighborhoods were far less segregated by color than they appear to be now, and on both Mitchell Street and City Park Avenue the Tatums had white neighbors, and white friends, as well as black."

When asked about racial tension, they both replied that the churches protected them and they were reared right, not to fuss. "In the early thirties [Jim] Butler's house on Tecumseh was on an all-white street. They helped us understand the conditions of blacks during that time." Although they made less money at that time, according to Butler and Herron, they lived better without welfare. Jim changes the subject (embarrassed). He doesn't want to talk about his accomplishments, they continue...

Gladys: The church music that he played.

Jim: My daddy asked him to play some church songs. He played "In the Shade of an Old Apple Tree" and sat Herman on his feet. That Art Tatum was something else!

Gladys: He was a beautiful person.

Jim: A lot of these great artists are temperamental, but not him. He was the same all the time.

Gladys: Even when he would come home he was the same, beautiful.

Jim: You couldn't spend no money in the club. Buy everybody drinks and just laugh and talk and have a good time.

Interview of Mary Belle Shealy

Introduction

Mary Belle Shealy was born January 13, 1911. She was also a pianist. She has been a piano teacher for many years in Toledo. Her experiences help us assess some of the stories about Tatum's Toledo. However, her life intersected with Tatum's only once; her knowledge of him as a musician performing in both white and black environments contributes interesting insights into the social history of Tatum's immediate community. She was two years younger than Tatum. She contributes an interesting comparison of her experiences as a young pianist in Toledo in the early twentieth century, suggesting what also might have been Tatum's experiences.

Shealy was interviewed in her home in March 20, 1992. She lives in what used to be in the early fifties and late sixties the major section of Toledo's black middle class. She grew up in the 400 block of Vance Street of the Pinewood District.[52] She moved to Toledo in 1917 when she was six years old. Walking with the help of a cane, Mary Belle ushered me into her living room where she sat near a window across from her piano. During our interview, as is the custom of someone who lives alone and has grown accustomed to

---

[52] See Introduction

waiting and watching, she frequently looked out of the window as if she was expecting someone. Like many of the interviews in this chapter, her memory of Tatum had already been jarred by the recent publicity. She frequently would refer to many of these publicized events or people.

Although she was willingly to talk, I felt many times that I was not synchronized with Shealy who had lived during a different period. When we discussed the nightlife of blacks she seemed to speak with caution as if she was guarding some secret. I later related this to Casey Jones' observation on what was and was not discussed.[53] She said during the interview that her memory was fine and indeed it would have to be for her to be teaching piano.

Musically, Shealy provides a bridge for the lay person who is interested in Toledo's black musical history and Tatum's music. She explains the transition of jazz from the dance music that Tatum played to the avant-garde or free form music that we have come to associate with musicians the likes of Bird and Dizzy Gillespie. Likewise, Shealy contributes to our knowledge of what her colleague, Tatum, probably experienced as a young man playing jazz piano in Toledo.

---

[53] See Casey Jones Interview.

Edited Taped Interview:

Shealy: I was born January 13, 1911 in Houston, Texas. There were very few blacks in Toledo at that time. I can remember in Houston that the blacks migrated coming North and I can remember my grandfather saying to my father, "Go North son so you can sleep and eat with the white folks."

Interviewer: Do you remember the Tatum family when you first came?

Shealy: No, I didn't know them. In fact, I didn't know them at all until one day I used to play in bands, you know, and so some of the musicians brought him over to my house. I didn't know him personally.

Interviewer: What night clubs did blacks have then?

Shealy: None in '33. See, I was 22 years old in 1933. That's the end of prohibition and then they started little clubs. I played in them. I played in hotels and clubs. Everywhere. I played in the church for blacks. I played all around and that was in '33. What was back in the twenties, I don't know because I was in school. I taught music when I was in high school. They couldn't pay for the music so I would play. I can remember the fellas asking my mother if I could go to nightclubs. First nightclub I played in was over on the eastside. I have played in the best clubs and the worst clubs. I taught the best children. Yeah. I had the majority of the blacks. I think I'm the only black teacher that teaches music like this. See, I don't teach in schools. For years I had all the professionals, Judge Franklin's sons and Stanley's [Cowell] folks.[54]

Interviewer: Do you still teach eight pupils?

Shealy: Um hum.

Interviewer: So they all come here now.

Shealy: They always came here. See, I haven't taught in schools. I didn't have the credentials to teach in schools. Now I have a piano teacher's certificate from the Sheridan Music School but I always taught in my house. I used to live on Vance Street before the urban renewal moved us out here and then I taught here.

Interviewer: Did you ever play at the Waiters and Bellmans?

Shealy: That's what I'm talking about, we called it the Musicians Club. Oh, yes. I played there a lot. We played the best ones. I've played out here at Inverness. One night at the Inverness the piano player walked out and they brought in a white artist then that played semi-classical music and I can remember this good looking white girl. Tall, stately and her name was Evelyn, I think. She played the violin and they couldn't find anybody that could read music. So one of the fellas knew I could read music and I saved their

---

[54] Dr. John Scott, personal interview, 15 September 1993. Professor John Scott, a longtime friend of Stanley Cowell's, remembered that Shealy taught Cowell and many others to play piano.

154

jobs. They had to come and get me and see, and that man he didn't like woman piano players. They didn't have anybody and so, honey, they brought me in there and I was fatter than this---I weighed about 300, and you know, where the Inverness Club is? Those fellas treated me so bad because they didn't know me. Al Fox was a violinist and they didn't even speak to me. They didn't speak to me when he brought me in there and, honey, I got up on this box because they had a little small stage, see men could get up on it easy but they had to help me up on this little stage and, honey, I could read that music. You talk about the things that you have to be subjected to. When I went to high school I played in the orchestra at Woodward. They had more than one pianist so they examined who could read the best. Well, they didn't really want me to be one of the pianists. But you know, I had music teachers that didn't teach me the fine art of piano. But I count and I made my students count. When the time come for me to be examined she threw me a difficult march in there, it had difficult changes but no problem. I could just look at it and read. So that's what you had to do. Those guys treated me terrible but when I saved their jobs for them it made a difference.

Interviewer: Did you see Tatum when he played at LaSalle's?[55]

---

[55] Porter 79. Although Porter records the building of boom of downtown Toledo in the 1920s, she does not include the musical affairs that Shealy refers to here. Porter

Shealy: No. I remember they brought him over to my house. It didn't affect me because he was just another piano player because the fellas told me how he could play, because I didn't think he was famous. He just played, you know what I mean. Honey, none of them affected me. I am telling you. Because this is how I feel. All of us have a mission. We all have something that we can contribute. So none of them affect me. I don't care how great they are. Most of them are lovely people. When we get through playing they always brought me home. The men would fool around and jam with each other. See they know about jamming so they should be able to give you a lot of information about Art Tatum. But I didn't---they always did---I played because at that time my friends would do domestic [work] and I could make more money playing the piano. My mother didn't want me to play in nightclubs. She had to spend her money to give me music so that's what I did. But, no, those fellas can tell you. If you can contact Perry's father and his brother, Mozart, they can tell you. Because we are about the same age. Now, I might be maybe two years older than they are, something like that... The only thing I had my knee operated and I cannot walk, but, honey, I get

---

writes that "the Lasalle and Koch Company had built a new store at the corner of Huron and Adams streets in 1917 and in 1927 they add three more floors." Clearly, blacks did play at white affairs and apparently this was another occasion. The WSPD radio was broadcasted from LaSalle's according to Toledo Public Local History Department's notes.

around. See some of my students think because I'm an old lady, I can't think, but my intelligence is still pretty sharp. We knew he could play. I think he left here. Didn't some white girl get him to play for her and that was the beginning?

Interviewer: I called the Toledo Musicians Union to maybe find out who taught Tatum.

Shealy: Honey, no, nobody taught Tatum, not of the piano teachers. I think he went to... Didn't he go to...? Didn't they send him some place, you know, like Columbus, some place like that? But I don't think anybody taught him music. I know... now I just read in my material that we have a man now who's teaching vision-impaired people. No piano teachers that we, you know, heard of. Because, see just like years ago what was his name, Garner boy--he's outstanding like Stanley... Then there's Pat, you know him don't you, Tony Patton? He'll be coming back here... to play Gershwin--he's done it before with the orchestra. He's in Alabama. He wanted a different teaching position so he's down there teaching. See we all knew the teacher that taught them. No, honey, no, long as I been in business, piano business, nobody taught Tatum. No Ma'am. See Tatum is my age so I should know, shouldn't I?

Interviewer: Did you belong to the Musicians Union?

Shealy: I had to belong to it for awhile. When you play in places like Kasey's to get by see how did I get by? See, those days were something else, I forget. But I knew I had to belong to it. The secretary was my friend, the black secretary.[56] He's dead now, too. Yeah, but I had to belong to it, yeah, because they pull you off the job. But the black union just phased out, they wouldn't do very much. The black guys couldn't get jobs with the white fellas. As I said, the men could tell you. Because I never asked for a job in my life. Someone always got me a job. I could play by music. They needed somebody to play by music.

Interviewer: Did they pay you the same as they paid the white musicians?

Shealy: I don't know. It's a scale. I can't remember because see so many white people played. See we played different joints, we played at white joints, played at the black joints and I think the best places. I don't know. See most jobs, we called gigs. Yes sir, I'm telling you, nickel beers.

Interviewer: Nickel beer?[57]

Shealy: Yeah. Nickel beers. I remember. I worked for a man and he told me, he said "You know, they don't think I make money." His name was Ed and he said, "You know, when your cash register rings nickels from 5 a.m. in the morning till one, then that's a lot of nickels." And it is. I can remember we thought back there, back

---

[56] See Harold Payne Interview.
[57] See Casey Jones and Harold Payne Interviews.

there we were making $5 a week. Doing domestic work some of them didn't make $3. Honey, I was knocking, wait a minute, at that time we would average about $29 a week, but you see, the thing about it, we got tips. And so they see I didn't drink so I always stayed sober, so you know I guess I had a pretty good personality, and they'd give us quarters. I'd get them quarters, and honey, at night we'd count them quarters up, that's a whole lot of quarters, you know that?

I can remember that first place I played; I had to play from dusk to dawn. Not all the time. Lots of times on Saturday from dusk to dawn. Me being the pianist the other instruments stopped but I couldn't stop. I mean the pianist had to keep going. But, honey, I had to. That was a whole lot of money back then. I can remember the first time I made $50. My mother worked in Commodore Perry's laundry. My mother used to pay half of her check for my music. We had to pay more and so they would tell us how silly they thought she was to sacrifice like that for me to take music. And so when I started I made $50 a week my mother got some of that.

I always was gonna go to Ohio State [University] but she didn't have enough money to send me to Ohio State, but I had this talent for the piano. Anyway, folks got where they couldn't pay for piano lessons, so I went to Philadelphia since I knew I could finish beauty culture in six months. I came back here and I was a beautician and played the piano. Honey, I had plenty of money because I was a beautician in the daytime and then I played for the white folks at night. I'm a mess. Oh, I had money because I had built up a nice beauty work clientele, and on Friday and Saturday night they said go on a gig at such and such a place. Honey, I'd go on that gig and I'd have plenty of money. Yes, sir. Then in '44 I started teaching music again, you know, when things started to pick up. But I've always been lucky. I think it's because I could play.

I got to tell you this. I used to play clubs, I mean just like the sororities and things, nice colored clubs would have affairs. They would hire us to play. So many people knew me. You know when we had intermission, honey, I can remember some of the ladies that were maids. Maids went and told my black boss to tell me not to associate with the guests. If I told you who some of those folks were, I think you would know some of them. Yeah. The help did not associate with the guests. Some of them were ashamed of me. I mean all of that is honest work, but the thing about it is I wasn't good enough, you know. It was beneath them. They weren't supposed to talk to me. People are funny. So I have really had some experiences in my life.

Interviewer: How did they respond to jazz or did you play jazz? What kind of music did you play?

Shealy: Classical. In fact, no piano teachers teach jazz. I mean maybe in the last ten years, but, honey, nobody teaches jazz... You just had style. They're what you call improvisation, but most teachers just teach you standard music. Because one thing about it, you got to have it within you or you cannot play. They can teach you how to improvise, teach you how to do this with that chord, how to do that with that chord, honey, it just doesn't have it. Honey, we have played it, but, you know, we didn't even call it jazz. I think, that's where it really got all mixed up because jazz in my dictionary, it tells you that jazz is the kind of music you can dance to, but the kind of jazz Tatum and them played you can't dance to it. See and that's what really gets to me. I can't understand it. And when it, something about it, you know, and have studied it, they say that music from Africa, you know, that we came from Africa, that music was functional, it served a purpose. So when we were here we danced to it. Music is something we danced to and that's how it carried over from Africa. Then when it got to Tatum and Jelly Roll Morton you didn't dance, you sat and listened. Now it becomes something that we listen to.

You know, I can't, I want to know how they really separate that unless you're going to call it contemporary jazz. When Stanley was writing, this concerto to jazz was written dum, de, dum, de, dum, de dum. Okay, but now when you listen they'll play this rhythm here and that rhythm there and I didn't like the concert because I mean when I went there I was looking for something like that.

Can you see, they don't count to jazz. They say, "Stanley you are composing jazz concerto." He said that is what they say. He did but I don't want to say it's a jazz concerto. I just want to say it's a piano concerto. I just don't understand that.

To me jazz is when you get rhythm and this jazz doesn't have that. Billy Taylor and Ramsey Lewis... that's jazz, honey, because it really had a rock to it. But to me, the concert stuff that Stanley plays is almost like Beethoven and Mozart. Yeah. Because you got to listen. Another thing about jazz. The jazz they talk about, I, you had no trouble identifying it. You know, just like when somebody plays "Stardust," you know it was "Stardust." Somebody played "Tea for Two"--like that.

I don't recognize anything in Tatum. You know what I mean? I have to listen and then I'll find out what his main melody is. Yeah, I just don't understand it. I hope one day you'll tell me what the difference in this jazz is because to me jazz as a dichotomy says music that you dance to which means it has a regular beat.

Interview of Harold Payne

Introduction

Harold Payne talked about Tatum's concern for others. Harold also referred to the Pinewood District where Tatum grew up as the "Silk Stocking Grove." His narrative on Toledo's black community, like Butler and Herron's, contains many of the names of people in Tatum's community, like a dancer and a female police officer, and Payne also remembers other forms of entertainment that were available to blacks. He also knew many of the musicians who came to Toledo. He remembered the effect that Jelly Roll Morton had on Toledo. But he, too, remembered Tatum's Toledo as strongly impacted by racism.

Payne contributes to our knowledge of Tatum's community and helps us to better understand Tatum's lifestyle and Tatum's feelings about his community.

Edited Oral Taped Interview:

Payne: After he [Tatum] got up in big money even here in Toledo the Lantern Club wanted him. So he told them, . . . "the only way I'll play is if my own people come in and see" and blacks couldn't go to any of these clubs. They couldn't even put their foot in unless they were waiting table or mopping floors, that's all. He said now if you allow my people to come in maybe two weeks, I'll play the job. Because he said, "I don't know when I'll be back to Toledo." He sensed that though, I guess, because he never did come back. That was the last time he played in Toledo. You know why they booked him there? It seated 4,000. That was the seating and the cost was cheap for him. Well, if Liberace played a job in Las Vegas for $50,000 a week and of course, Liberace was a different type, you see he is concert, but Art wasn't. He was just naturally jazz. A lot of people say blues, but he wasn't a blues piano player, he was jazz. Blues piano player because he died when he was young, was called Jelly Roll Morton.

Interviewer: Were there a lot of musicians, poets, and artists in Toledo?

Payne: Well, musicians, yeah and stage shows, too. Like "Jimmy Cooks Review," called "Black and Tan," you see that was burlesque. Well there were two different shows, a white show and black shows. The white shows were performed first and then the next half was the black performers because they had the best shows. The first half must have got wise to it because if the blacks went on first, well, the whites wouldn't want to see the white show because it didn't have the black talent they had. There wouldn't be nobody there looking for the last shows and same way when they brought

"Shuffle Along" in.[58] That was the greatest road show that ever hit the road.

What is implied in these interviews is that black Americans and, in particular, famous blacks like Art Tatum have suffered oppression from the years of racial oppression. Therefore, it can be concluded from Casey's interview that Tatum was a success in his community because he was a musician.[59]

Images of Tatum

Toledo's black community, in retrospect, was more protected and form closer ties with their neighbors and family than today according to all of the informants in this chapter. How this affected Tatum is obvious. In a community that looked after each other, Tatum experienced a sense of freedom and independence during his years in Toledo that is uncommon today. This was not all

---

[58] Leronne Bennett, Before the Mayflower (Penguin Books: Baltimore Maryland, 1961) 390. "Shuffle Along," first of a series of popular musicals featuring Negro talent, opened at the 63rd Street Musical Hall New York City, May 23, 1921. Where it played in Toledo cannot be documented.

[59] Lester 41. Smith writes that it was not until recently and 1988 in particular when they put on a Art Tatum Day that the city of Toledo began to give Tatum any recognition. However, no one came to the Art Tatum Day which suggests that Tatum's name in the black community in 1920s and 30s meant something different from the public recognition that is commonly associated with a jazz musician of Tatum's magnitude in other communities. Casey's interview seems to define that relationship.

good. The early morning incident involving the loss of his vision was an example. Also, this closeness in the black community resulted in an indifference to Tatum. Casey regrets that he did not pay more attention to Tatum's playing and Butler and Herron remembered that he just played for them at parties without realizing the depth of his talent.

Toledo's black community provided Tatum with his first audiences. Their acceptance of him gave him the confidence that he needed to continue to play and develop the style that made him famous. Likewise, the instrument that Tatum selected and the culture milieu of the black community during this time helped to create the Tatum style. Because a piano was the most popular and often the only instrument available at house parties, Tatum played the whole orchestra (stride piano).

Although they did not have anything to compare him to, Herron and Butler remembered that he was good and always willing to play. Tatum enjoyed playing the piano. If there was a piano and Tatum, Herron remembered that they were going to have some music. He never seemed to get tired of playing because his fans, according to Herron and Butler, never had to beg him to play. His sense of humor and friendliness was also part of his style. This kind of clowning seems normal for a young man.

Shealy, another pianist playing during the same time as

Tatum, documents the struggles of other musicians in Toledo. Her backdrop to those years shed light on the eclecticism that occurred among blacks and whites. Shealy played with bands who were required to play and read classical music for white social occasions at country clubs and local night spots. This created a racial mix. Lois Nelson said that she moved between both communities, her white community and the Bohemian community created by prohibition. On the surface, this made things appear as if there was no racial tension. Other informants (Tana Porter, Toledo Profile and LeRoy Williams, Black Toledo) stated that there was a separation between black and white social events, community institutions and neighborhoods.

It was physically impossible for Tatum to play for all occasions. Other musicians, like Shealy, had those opportunities that Tatum declined. Tatum, however, played at both black and white affairs. Unlike Shealy, his popularity allowed him to be selective and independent of financial pressures. Both Tatum and Shealy, however, had to cope with the gangsters who controlled the clubs. Shealy also suggested that there was a class eliticism operating in the black community. She recalls that many of her black neighbors would not speak to her when she played for them at their social affairs. Although she wanted to attend college, her jobs as a pianist, beautician, and teacher paid well enough for her to provide for herself and her mother.

Shealy's experiences highlight two sets of black Toledoans impacting the development of young black adults. "Old-styled," or established upper middle professional families such as the Stewarts and Gordons, having resided in Toledo for several generations, built the institutions in the black community. They fostered the new young adult migrant, lower middle class, blue-collar workers whose children composed the second generation, like Shealy and Tatum. It was probably these "old-styled" families who were the founders of the churches that Butler and Herron refer to. It is not clear from the data, however, how Tatum really felt about the Stewarts, but Ella P. Stewart, in her memoirs, clearly stated that she believed Tatum owed her and her husband.

All of Tatum's contemporaries in this chapter broke from some of the traditions already established within the black community and vis-à-vis, the black church. Casey remembers that everyone went to the after-hours, but it was not something you talked about. Shealy experienced snobbery because she worked as a musician. Butler and Herron recalled that it was the black church that socialized them. This was the kind of class dynamic that impacted Tatum's life in Toledo and caused his drinking and music to be accepted by some of his friends and family as the natural result of change within the black community.

Tatum was known only as a fun-loving and friendly person who could play the piano. Casey defined Tatum as 'a man and his music' which also explains Tatum's relationship with his community. Lester Smith, Too Marvelous for Words, writes that it was not until recently when they sponsored an Art Tatum Day in 1988 that the City of Toledo began to acknowledge Tatum's genius. However, no one came to that event, suggesting that Tatum's name in the black community in the twenties and thirties meant something different from the public recognition that is commonly associated with a jazz musician of Tatum's magnitude in other communities.[60] Tatum's fellow musicians, however, were well aware of his talents.

---

[60] Lester 41.

CHAPTER FOUR

Tatum and Other Toledo
Musicians

Here, we are going to be expanding on the origins of Tatum's musicianship utilizing interviews from within the Toledo's musical community and to continue documentation. The oral taped interviews in this chapter are from musicians who knew Tatum in Toledo or played with him before he left with Adelaide Hall for New York in June 1932.[1] It seems important to consider Tatum's musical community and occupation separately from his family, friends, and neighbors.

This chapter focuses on the Tatum's stage image and how it differs from that of the private Tatum. It also documents that his public image is subject to change depending on the informants' individual perceptions. For example, his image is perceived by lay people as a local pianist who played for the love of it more than for income. However, his peers in music entertainment remember him

---

[1] Many of the primary documents, such as a bill to William Stewart, a letter from Bert Hicks (Adelaide Hall's husband) in the Toledo Public Library's files, and a telegram from Bert Hicks to William Stewart speak to this much contested date.

as having had a keen sense for business and a level-headedness sufficient to demand fair remuneration for his services. Ben Webster, a musician, recalls:

He wanted Tatum to sit in on a set, but Tatum (according to Randle) didn't like to play for nothing, at least not in a commercial club. Webster finally prevailed, by giving Art a hundred-dollar bill. Tatum checked to make sure it wasn't a ten.[2]

However, in Toledo where he cultivated his unique talent, friends like Gladys Herron (referred to in Chapter III) remember "his enthusiasm for playing anywhere, anytime, and under any circumstance." Musicians such as Harold Payne who knew Tatum in Toledo, referred frequently to Tatum's generosity at rent parties in the twenties and thirties. As biographer James Lester has noted, there was a difference in Tatum's response to the commercial world and his people in the after-hours.[3]

Tatum's public and private lives with women are also subject to speculation. It is obvious that he enjoyed the company of women. Lester further remarks:

Women were not absent from Art's later life (his illegitimate son [Orlando] was born when he was twenty-four, and later he was twice married), but for the biographical record he must have

---

[2] Lester 181.
[3] Lester 106-7.

entered his twenties with lots of experience at the piano and very little experience with women.[4]

Likewise, Eddie Barefield, a musician who lived near Tatum in the early 1930s, tells a story about sitting at a bar with Art and having Art interrupt the conversation to move closer to an attractive woman who had sat down some distance away.[5] Also in a picture with Beryle Brooker, a female entertainer, taken in 1947, Tatum is sitting closest to her and is looking very admiringly at her. In this picture Tatum does not appear to be shy. In fact, out of seven men he is the only one looking at her and smiling.[6] There was also talk that Billie Holiday, a popular black singer of the thirties, loved him.[7] Sylvia Sims, a popular singer in the forties, remembered Tatum affectionately. Her insight is invaluable because through her conversations with James Lester, she brings to our discussion additional understanding of Tatum's relationship with women:

I had those big long braids wrapped around my head, for which he named me Moonbeam Moskowitz. I had very long, long hair and it had never been cut, and I guess the first time Arthur ever met me he pulled my braid and said, "Are you an Indian?" I said, "No, I'm from Brooklyn," and he said, "oh, you're a Jewish Indian," and he

---

[4] Lester 30.
[5] Lester 25.
[6] Lester. Centerfold (Frank Driggs Collection).
[7] Lester 161.

named me Moonbeam Moskowitz. I guess you could not, I at least could not get inside Arthur. But I know he adored me, and I know he adored the fact in my own virtue I was Great, greatly innocent... I guess maybe it was kind of refreshing to him. He was extremely generous... Arthur never made passes at me. I don't know what would have happened if he had--but I think he was more amused by me than in love with me.

Arthur always gave me these--they used to make these little pianos then, see he had a friend who was a glass-spinner... He knew somebody who did that, and he gave me one once and then it got broken... The next thing that Arthur gave me, for my birthday, was a kind of charm, a gold piano, from Van Cleef--Oh, God, it was so many years ago.[8]

Although Sims refers to Tatum after he left Toledo in 1932, he didn't seem at that time to be shy, inexperienced, or awkward with her. In fact, Russell Cowan, a Toledo musician, and others seem to not have noticed Tatum's romances. Tatum's relationships with women certainly reveal the problem we encounter when trying to discern the man from the musician. The public Tatum attracted considerable attention, but how this manifested itself in his private life cannot be documented. Women, for example, as with today's groupies, could have been seeking money, love, or fame. Women's

---

[8] Lester 161-2.

motives, details of his relationship with Marnette Jackson, the circumstances of his divorce from Ruby Arnold, or his life with Geraldine Williamson are unknown. The few details that exist are detailed through the accounts of other musicians or friends and not the women themselves. The problem is all too well defined by Harold Payne, who said, "You see I wasn't with him all the time..."

Even in the early years, because of his style of music, Tatum's image among musicians was different from the general public's image of him and the music. Jack Jackson explained:

But I think what his hardest problem was, I believe, was that he was so advanced that the people didn't quite understand him. You see he was low. The only people that really dug him was musicians. You never heard no layman talk about him. Hell, they didn't know anything and very few musicians did, but they knew something...[9]

The following interviews address these points and increase our insight into Toledo's musical community and the Tatum image.

---

[9] "Art Tatum: The Art of Jazz Piano."

Toledo's Musical Community

According to the people interviewed for this study, books, and Toledo's journals and newspapers, Toledo's musical community did not differ radically from those in other towns in the United States during the jazz era. The major players in both Toledo's white and black entertainment communities were the musicians and the underworld gangsters, owners of the brothels and clubs. Harry Illman writes in his controversial work, <u>Unholy Toledo</u>, that after the prohibition was enacted the "new social order saw the birth of speakeasies and the rise of organized gangs [who controlled] the highly profitable bootlegging business."[10] However, in Toledo there were very few clubs that admitted blacks for any purpose other than to entertain. The most popular black club, according to many of the black musicians interviewed for this study, was the Waiters and Bellmans Club (see Chapter III) which was operated by Johnny Crocket. Crocket was said to be connected with the underworld, allowing him to operate 24 hours a day. Located on Indiana Avenue, a popular section of Toledo's black Pinewood District, the Waiters and Bellmans Club attracted many famous musicians. Some came to hear a young pianist named Tatum play and others came through

---

[10] Illman 97.

Toledo on their way to or from major musical centers, like Detroit, Chicago, and Cleveland.

During the prohibition era, Toledo followed the national trend.[11] Prominent speakeasies replaced former bars. The Villa, Tabernilla, Chateau La France and Casino were "leading hangouts" according to Illman.[12] Although Tatum performed in many of these establishments, they did not embrace him as a customer. Later there were other black clubs in which Tatum was alleged to have played. The Green Lantern and Charlie's Chicken Shack were two of the other clubs mentioned.[13] However, for Tatum there were other places where he would sharpen his musical talents. The places most often mentioned by Tatum biographers were Toledo's after-hours clubs/joints.

The after-hours or "after-hours joints," which had certain characteristics and functions within the black community, have been documented in Katrina Hazzard-Gordon's book Jookin.[14] She describes an after-hours joint as a club: willing to stay open after other places closed in accord with the law. After-hours joints ranged

[11] Ogren 5. Ogren writes that "the audience for jazz was advertently stimulated when Congress passed the Volstead Act, which banned the manufacture and sale of alcoholic beverages, in 1919.
[12] Illman 96.
[13] According to notes made by an unknown librarian in the Toledo Public Library Local History Department file on Art Tatum, in 1928 Tatum played with Speedy Webb at Charlie's Chicken Shack and was replaced by Fritz Weston.
[14] Katrina Hazzard-Gordon, Jookin (Philadelphia: Temple University Press, 1990).

widely in decor and atmosphere, but most offered drinking, dancing, music, food and sometimes gambling... The after-hours joint was in one sense a business establishment, a characteristic it shared with saloons, honky-tonks, and dance halls. Few charged an admission price, but once inside the participants were expected to pay for practically everything. Only the dancing was free, at least until coin-operated music appeared. Before the invention of jukeboxes, the source of music ranged from individual musicians to piano rolls and old Victrolas. A musician's services could always be enlisted for a plate of food or drinks; sometimes musicians would play for free.[15]

She continues that "after-hours joint like the street lottery known as the numbers [racket], became an important element in the underground business structure of black Americans."[16] The after-hours joints in Toledo, as in other cities, were a result of racial segregation of and increased leisure time that blacks experienced as a result of their migration to northern cities--northern economy's prosperity provided more recreational time. Although leisure time was available to blacks, integrated recreation was rarely a fact of life.

As a consequence, blacks began their own forms of recreation, emulating the Southern jook joints, which resulted in the after-hours joints.

---

[15] Hazzard-Gordon 89.
[16] Hazzard-Gordon 91.

Another form of social gatherings for African Americans from the 1900s to the 1920s was the rent party or shout. According to Hazzard-Gordon, "the rent parties were a way to pay the rent and originated... [when] a black person had to pay his rent and couldn't. The rent party stems from two divergent traditions: the jook and the church social..."[17] Rent parties operated through the assistance of others who invested in their neighbor's party as insurance against their own future hard times: If I attend and pay at yours perhaps you will do the same for me! Hazzard-Gordon writes that:

jook joints was generally furnished by a musician on a piano or guitar. According to interviews I [Hazzard-Gordon] conducted, the musician would usually play for a good meal and all the liquor he could drink. Apparently, musicians considered the "rent shout circuit" an excellent arena in which to hone their skills. Stiff competition, one musician after another would take his turn demonstrating his skill. This practice spilled over from the honky-tonks, jooks, and after-hours joints, but its roots go back to Africa, where such competitions are still common.[18]

Toledo also seemed to have its share of rent parties to which Tatum and other musicians contributed their talents. Interviewees like Harold Payne, Gladys Herron, and Jim Butler mentioned Tatum's

---

[17] Hazzard-Gordon 96-97.
[18] Hazzard-Gordon 96-97.

enthusiasm at these events. Likewise, Tatum's repetition as a stiff competitor at cutting contests, all-night musical competitions, have been documented by Felicity Howlett in her dissertation. Jack Jackson, a Toledo musician, defines Tatum's enthusiasm as 'ego.' According to Jackson:

I tell you one thing about him, he was egotistical this way. You know every time he would go around piano players they would always scatter. He would stand right up to them. But when they would come up and tell him say--have you heard this guy?--this kind of got to him, you know. He wanted to hear who the guy was. They were telling him about Bud Powell, so he went and heard Bud Powell and the first thing he told Bud Powell was "You don't have a left hand." You know he played modern piano. So they tell me that Bud Powell went in the woodshed for about six months. You know he studied some tune and then got his left hand and so when Tatum came back to town he went to hear him again. He was kind of getting back at Tatum so he was playing and he was playing his left hand. Tatum told him when he got through playing, "Listen to this." So he started playing "Tea for Two." When he got over it, I think you have heard this one, when he got over into about the third course he started playing "It Ain't Necessarily So" on his left hand and "Tea For Two" on his right hand and that did it, you know. He said try this some time. I tell you, he was unbelievable. He would run you up the wall. I tell you it's a thing like this--Babe Ruth for a long time was home runs and nobody even threatened him. Now can you imagine what would happen if somebody was chasing him. His 50 and 60 home runs come natural you know, what do you think he would have tried, same way with Tatum. You see like, if you pushed him you see. Now that to me showed that he was sort of egotistical. Like I said everywhere he go, they just scattered, you know.[19]

All of these social gatherings, as well as the church, helped shape Tatum's style and talent.

Although Ohio, and Toledo in particular, may not be included in "Downbeat" or other jazz magazines as a state or city popular for its jazz musicians or music, in Tatum's time Ohio was known for its jazz by musicians. According to Garvin Bushnell's, Jazz From The Beginning:

Ohio produced a lot of jazz musicians. McKinney's Cotton Pickers came out of Springfield. Ted Lewis was from Circleville. Willis and Wormack were in Dayton, so was John Brown, of Brown's Syncopators. Vic Dickenson came out of Zenia. Of course, Columbus had better musicians than Springfield --Slam Stewart, the pianist, led bands there. But trombonist Quentin "Butter" Jackson came out of

---

[19] "Art Tatum: The Art of Jazz Piano"

Springfield, as did Claude Jones, who taught him, and Earle Warren of the Basie band.[20]

Tatum was not alone in Ohio in his interest in jazz or devil's music (a name coined by a class-conscious member of the African American community during this period for music other than spirituals).[21] Musicians such as Garvin Bushnell, were also listening to rag. Rag music was initially developed by black musicians for the entertainment of their own people and was a precursor to jazz.[22] Garvin writes that:

Ragtime piano was the major influence in that section of the country. Everybody tried to emulate Scott Joplin. The change began to come around 1912 to 1915, when the four-string banjo and saxophone came in. About the first tenor saxophonist anyone in that area heard was Milt Senior, who played with Willis and Womack, and eventually joined McKinney's. Negroes in Springfield [Ohio] were very aware of popular music as part of their life.[23]

---

[20] Garvin Bushnell, Jazz from the Beginning (Ann Arbor: University of Michigan Press, 1990) 10.

[21] James Cone, The Spirituals and the Blues (New York: The Seabury Press, 1972) 111.

[22] Eileen Southern, The Music of Black Americans (New York: W.W. Norton, 1983) 308.

[23] Bushnell 10.

Tatum was to later play with Milt Senior.[24] Tatum does not allude to Scott Joplin's influence. He does, however, acknowledge Fats Waller as his primary inspiration, and refers to popular pianist

---

[24] Mayola Senior, personal interview with John Cleveland, 11 November 1981. According to Mayola:

> Art Tatum was gifted and played anything he heard... He could improvise and would add to, but when he was with my late husband's band at the Chateau and Tontea, that name is as close as I remember, I do not remember him ever composing anything. My late husband Milton Senior always said that the band had to follow Art. This presented some difficulty for any soloist to appear with the band or ensemble even at WSPD radio station where they appeared twice a week. Art loved the piano. Milton often had to go looking for him when it was time to go to work. He would find him someplace he had played all night for nothing or anything they would give him or doing something I never understood, playing cards.

> Also, he seemed to be able to differentiate between a high denomination bill waved before his face and a low one. This was when a patron would be asking him for a certain number at the club. In later years, Tatum may have been very well compensated for his talent as he moved from Toledo to New York City. I do not remember him returning unless very briefly to visit his family. In my estimation, he would have trouble playing with a big band, but could always appear as a guest artist like some of the current blind talent artists today. My late husband's band was one of the first jazz ensembles to appear in Toledo. Only four instruments playing, perhaps it was prohibition that forced the big bands out and smaller night club groups in where the demand was more for talented individual musicians. Musicians during those days shunned Toledo and if they played a one-night stand there they would leave immediately for Detroit. Other black musicians had to travel to make money. TV bands and so forth were only for the white ones with no blacks in their bands so it was hard to get good musicians or to have them sign a contract.

Lee Sims, "whose interpretations contained many interesting harmonics... [Tatum said he was] a secondary influence."[25] Tatum and his inspired teacher, Fats Waller, later became good friends. About this friendship Lester wrote:

Tatum, I think found a real soul-mate in Fats Waller, perhaps the only one he ever found. They lived alike (namely, as high as their income would allow), drank alike (almost constantly), and shared similar attitudes toward the piano [both had impeccable technique and a leaning toward more serious music that largely was suppressed by their need to make a career in jazz].[26]

Other than his training at the Toledo School of Music, where he learned to read sheet music with the aid of glasses as well as by the Braille method, Tatum was virtually self-taught, learning from piano rolls, phonograph recordings, radio broadcasts, and various musicians whom he encountered as a young man in the area around Toledo and Cleveland, according to the New Grove Dictionary.[27] Lester writes that:

The new music was spread across the nation through the technology of radio and recording, which in the 1920s replaced the piano in the parlor as our main home entertainment. Recordings

---

[25] New Grove Dictionary 519.
[26] Lester 78.
[27] New Grove Dictionary 519.

played the role of teachers, as hundreds of future jazz musicians took their first steps by learning recorded solos, purely by listening... this was the decade in which Tatum's powers first began to develop. It shaped him, it defined the playing field on which he had to make his runs, and it provided him with a base of operations, namely, jazz.[28]

Toledo was Tatum's original playing field. As indicated in earlier chapters, Tatum played with bands and other musicians at black and white clubs. He became recognized for his tremendous talent early by commercial Toledo. "In 1927 when he was about eighteen years old, Tatum won a local amateur contest and as a result began appearing on Toledo's WSPD... Jon Hendricks (another famous Toledo entertainer) competed often in these local amateur contest which were a popular form of entertainment."[29] In the album notes of Art Tatum Piano Solo, David G. Hyltone writes that "Tatum's performance along with a friend, a vocalist, resulted in the offer of a job at station (WSPD). Art accepted but only after his friend had been given a job also."[30]

Tatum's departure from Toledo and his arrival in New York has been the source of confusion for biographers. Tatum worked in

---

[28] Lester 66.
[29] Lester 52.
[30] David G. Hyltone, Art Tatum Piano Solo, Decca Album No. A-585.

Toledo and the surrounding areas until he left with Adelaide Hall in 1932. A letter that was placed in the Toledo Public Library files in 1992 and a contract with Hall--signed 'X', with Tatum's name in print--collaborates the contention that Tatum played with Adelaide Hall (see Contract appended). While there appears to be some uncertainty regarding who left with Tatum, this letter clearly identifies Tatum as having a traveling companion. Ella P. Stewart's husband, William, was paid by Bert Hicks for being Tatum's manager. Lester argues in <u>Too Marvelous For Words</u> that amateur historians have distorted Stewart's role in Tatum's departure from Toledo. The contract and letter indicate Lester's incorrectness on this point. In her interview in the <u>Toledo Public Library's Oral Collection of African Americans in Toledo, Ohio</u>, Stewart reveals hurt and disappointment at Tatum's indifference to her and her husband's later visits to New York. She also discussed her role in bringing Tatum to the attention of Hall and Hicks, who were staying in a room above her pharmacy during their 1932 stay in Toledo.[31] Hall was responsible for Tatum's entrance onto the international stage.

Tatum's influence on local music and other musicians is apparent by the oral interviews in this chapter. Tatum certainly impressed his fellow musicians. Eddie Barefield, in a 1988 interview from the video, <u>Art Tatum: The Art of Jazz Piano</u> remembered this:

---

[31] See Ella P. Stewart Interview.

Tatum lived on City Park in Toledo and when I was in Toledo in 1932 I lived right across the street from him and he was about, maybe at that time about 17 or maybe he was a little older, maybe he was about 20 years old. He used to buy all of Earl Hines' records, because Earl Hines was one of his favorite musicians and when I first went there [to Toledo], I was musical director for Frank Terry's Chicago Nightingales, I was about 22 then. We used to play at the Recreation Ballroom and every Monday night we gave a colored dance, this Monday we were playing this dance and I had intermission and I was getting ready to go out and get me a drink or something and Frank says to me, "wait a minute I want you to hear something." I said, "What do you want me to hear?" I was anxious to get out. He says, "I want you to hear a pianist." I said, "Oh, I've heard all the piano players, I heard Earl Hines, Frank Hines, I heard Fats, I heard all these others, I don't need to hear nobody play now." As I was going out they put this blind kid up on a stand and he sat down. As I reached the door he made a big arpeggio on the piano and went into "Tiger Rag" on the piano. I switched and turned right around and went back up there to listen to him play and it was just fantastic.[32]

A rarely mentioned attribute of Tatum was his ability to form the bands needed both in his early Toledo years and later in his

---

[32] "Art Tatum: The Art of Jazz Piano."

famous California and New York trios. In 1924, an early Toledo ensemble that young Tatum assembled included Milton Senior, Harold Fox, Bill Moore, Lester Smith, and Fats Mason.[33]

Tatum was known as generous, loyal with his fellow musicians. Even during his early days in Toledo, Tatum was known as a patient teacher. Mary Lou Williams states that:

Art Tatum taught me how to control the keyboard with my hands. I used to hang out with him in Toledo and Cleveland when he was about eighteen. I'd play at a club while he was resting. When he sat down, I'd sit right next to him, imitate what I heard, and learned a lot of things that way.[34]

As previously stated by Hyltone, Tatum exhibited loyalty to his fellow entertainer. Lester corroborates that:

Alongside his independence Art always looked out for people he worked with, gave them advances whether they wanted them or not, and in other ways impressed his friends with his generosity. His friend Billy Fuster told me, "He was very congenial. Easy to get along with... Of course, he was well-liked, 'cause he always had a buck for somebody. He never was a tightwad." If he was making money he liked to spend it, even in his earliest days of

---

[33] Lester 48.
[34] Lyons 71.

making money out of music.[35]

Although Tatum was liked by his fellow musicians for his generosity and loyalty, it doesn't seem that his loyalty extended to the Toledo Federation of Musicians. Tatum was not a member of the musicians union, but the history of its development and its effect on Tatum and the other musicians during the years that Tatum was in Toledo can contribute to our understanding of Tatum.[36] This information on the union is not the focus of this study but it has been included in the following interviews.

Many of the musicians interviewed spoke of their awe upon hearing Tatum perform for the first time. Their interviews reveal many of the attitudes that surround the legend of Tatum. It is difficult to separate fact from fiction, but it is always the story of Tatum's that is most interesting. When we study these interviews we begin to see more of Tatum's personality, such as his willingness to teach, his patience with other musicians, and his ability to drink an enormous amount of alcohol without apparent negative effects on his playing. The letter addressed to the Stewarts from Hall's husband is one of the rare times that Tatum's use of alcohol was documented as a problem.[37] These details of Tatum's musical career

---

[35] Lester 65.

[36] Conversation on January 1991 with Mary Russo, president of the Toledo Federation of Musicians.

[37] See letter, Toledo Local History Library, Art Tatum File.

and public personality are revealed in the following documents and edited interviews.

Interview of Harold Payne

Introduction

The legend of Art Tatum can be traced to his earlier years in Toledo, Ohio when, at ten years old, the legends and myths about Tatum's musical genius began.   Harold Payne, 82 years old at interview date, was Tatum's age and a musician. Although not born in Toledo, Payne came to Toledo as a young child. He remembers hearing musicians talk about "this kid who played a loud piano." Payne was interviewed March 20, 1992 in his home in the upper class, predominantly white district of Toledo called Ottawa Hills. Although Payne was ill he consented to being interviewed, but he has since died. He was one of the few living musicians in Toledo who played with Tatum, and he "traveled as a musician for twenty years."

After ending his musical career, Payne opened a dry cleaning store in inner city Toledo and operated it "for about forty years." The author located Payne through a patron of Payne's Fashion Cleaners. This customer mentioned that if Art Tatum's name came up in conversation, Payne would talk for hours about him. He was right.

Payne's interview contains many anecdotes about Tatum. Many of these have been documented by others and some, like the surgery on Tatum's hand to extend his reach, have not. Payne's interview is valuable because we get a view of Tatum in Toledo that veers from the traditional, and we can get a sense of what he meant to other Toledo musicians. Sometimes Payne's reminiscences seem incoherent, but those who are familiar with Tatum's life and who do not need chronologically ordered details will find much delight in his personal account of Tatum's younger years as a musician in Toledo.

Edited Oral Taped Interview

Payne: I knew Art from being around, I just knew that he played piano though and at that age I just figured he was just another kid piano player. A lot of the guys would take him on the job and at intermission he would be out there playing marbles with some of the students. Oh, he was something.[38]

Interviewer: Did you actually hang out with Tatum?

---

[38] Lester 47. Lester writes that Tatum was probably being booked by club owners as early as fifteen or sixteen (1924-25).

Payne: Yeah, when I wasn't working. You see, I was working with different bands around here. A lot of times I got a job or else he would find one and wanted some musicians, he would come and send over after me. We worked together all right, but he was better off by himself. There are a lot of articles where during the depression, you know how things were then, things were bad, so people would get house rent parties. Blacks, you know, we never had any jobs back there then. We would get together this month and maybe you and I wanted to give a house rent party. We would make enough money at a party to pay rent, sell a little whiskey, bootleg whiskey. Art, when it was time for the party, he'd go. He said the reason why he'd go in and play there just because he wanted to help the people pay for the rent. He never charged them nothing. A lot of time people would tip him just to play, but he never charged nobody. He just wanted to see people make some money.

He played out to Toledo University at the senior prom and he didn't have a very big band, some of his men didn't get there, but it went over okay though.[39] Then he got a few jobs. You see, I wasn't playing, and I had other business. I was playing a few nights a week because I had a little band and worked three to four nights a week.

---

[39] Lester 48. This is probably the same occasion that Lester refers to. According to Payne, Tatum was to provide music for a dance but forgot. At the last minute Tatum hired two horn players who did not play because everyone wanted to hear Tatum.

You see, Art would say "Why don't you come with us?" I would say, "Man, I make more money in three nights than you guys make in a whole week." I was very lucky then in one of those bootleg places, you've heard of the gangsters in Toledo?[40]

> *Interviewer*: Licavoli?

> *Payne*: Yeah, because he had all of those places tied up. If you go in his place, money kept flowing in. Gangsters are like this-- your daughter didn't mean nothing to them. They worked like this. They would have bills stacked up like this [raising his hands about six inches from the table top] and go around singing at the tables. He would move you from tip to top bill. If it was a dollar it was yours, if it was a $5, $10 or $20 that was yours also.

> *Interviewer*: When he wasn't playing piano what did he do?

> *Payne*: When he could see a little bit he liked playing cards, whist, he and a fellow named Roselle. Roselle was cripple but he was not as bad as Art. They were good buddies. You see, Roselle could take a round, too, and when those guys get to playing whist nobody could beat them. They talked a lot of jive to each other. They said, "You wanna challenge us?" "Uh-uh," I said, "Keep your mouth shut I'll play." They knew I knew what he was doing, talking

---

[40] See Casey Jones and Gladys Herron Interview. Jones also describes in his interview the influence of the gangsters on Toledo's black community. For a detailed description of Toledo's involvement of gangsters in both the government and lives of Toledoans, see Harry Illman's Holy Toledo.

crazy, jive talk, until they knew every card in each other's hand. A lot of them [musicians] just played for a pasttime. In fact, they didn't have much money to go anywhere. Did you ever hear them advertise on television about these old numbers that came out in the sixties?

Interviewer: Yes.

Payne: There was a guy who said you can listen to all of the hit parades when they come on the radio, everybody listen to that and that was the only entertainment back there during the depression. Then you could take your wife out and almost go in a club all night long with a dollar. When beer first came in it sold for about 10 cents a bottle. Then they raised it to about 12 cents. Bootleg whiskey you could get a 50 cents pitcher. That was all over the country, all cities, because what could blacks do. They didn't have a WPA at that time and they had to do something to make it, clearinghouses and numbers and stuff, but what else was there to do?

Interviewer: Is that where he gained most of his experience?

Payne: Yes. He just liked to play. If he would go in a house, I don't care what, if a piano was there he would sit down and play. You know, that's all he could do.

Interviewer: Was that because everybody had a piano?

Payne: No, it wasn't that. They had what his sister would say, "If you touch that piano you'd better not hit any bad notes." Art could walk up to a piano and hit a bunch of keys and call the notes right off the notes he hit. He had a perfect ear. (That was what Arlene said in the Blade. They had a lot of the top piano players and musicians in there).

Interviewer: Was he gone from Toledo a long time to study Braille?

Payne: No, he studied right here in Toledo, then he went to Columbus, he might have went there.[41] You see I wasn't with him all the time, there wasn't a steady job hardly.

---

[41] Jack Jackson Interview, Cleveland. According to Cleveland:

This teacher that Tatum studied with, I know Bill was talking about him. [Jackson is probably talking about Bill Cummerow, another partially blind black pianist who took lesson from Tatum's early Jefferson School teacher, Overton G. Ramey. See Lester 38.] He said that it was required at school for the blind that you take piano because they thought that might be something he could make a living at and that was why, so everybody had to do that four years. They had to take it the whole time they were at school. Bill told me, he wouldn't put it on a tape, but he said about the whitey, he wasn't real strict about that. It was like take the lessons and Bill wasn't enthusiastic about taking them. The guy just put it down that Bill had come every Wednesday for four years and collected the money for teaching him--six months or so he never made the lessons, but the guy taught him to read Braille and taught him conventional theory. He taught him what the chords were. Bill didn't know too much about how to apply that theory. He played, he didn't do any improvisation although he did play some bars and something like that. Bill said that he did require them to learn that. Every now and then he would say "Have you

Interviewer: What about the Waiters and Bellmans Club?

Payne: We had all the best musicians in the country there. I think Duke [Ellington] was there. We invited him to a party and one of the fellows played trumpet was from Toledo and they were down there. We were at this party, I had a cup of tea and was singing with them--trying to drink a drink. Got down on the get down! You see Toledo was really a town at one time for music. We had the best musicians come through here. See it's what they call a 'rabbit town.' Yeah, big groups and everybody. You know they were the ones who had money, they had the ability to bring all the best attractions.

Payne: Here's what he said, he said he wouldn't play the job unless his own people were welcome to hear him. I said of course all of us musicians knew what was going to happen. White folks down there know who spends money and they seen how much money they spent--never did back out of it and then they all started to bring them in gradually. Our people spend a lot of money, I wonder why they do this and that. I said, "Look, we were down so long I say when we get the chance to make some money. You're gonna enjoy yourself."

Interviewer: Did they treat him okay?

---

heard Art Tatum?" Bill would say "Yeah." Said, "Well, you know he's wasting his talent. He's into jazz. He should be studying the classics."

Payne: Think of it like this, entertainers helped break segregation. That's when they started mixing, when they started to get mixed bands. At one time you never see no mixed bands, white and black. You see these white musicians the way they learned how to get a lot of stuff they hung around blacks so much they pretty soon were playing just like them.

Interviewer: Did the white musicians always hang around with blacks?

Payne: Yeah, everywhere. I said that's what broke up segregation and the entertainers, white and black entertainers.

Interviewer: Was this the same in Toledo?

Payne: No. Not as long as the Licavoli's controlled the place. No they never said anything. They never did have trouble with it. They were the ones that really started integration in the music. Duke Ellington had one of the top trombone players in the country and he was white. He had a few of them. A lot of say--how come they hired him? I said, "Give him credit." Now that's the top trombone player in the country that you can hear of and he begged a job from a black man, so you know they are beginning to recognize us. You notice here lately that all the bands you see now are mixed.

Interviewer: But they were mixed back then?

Payne: Yeah, they were gradually beginning to. You see white boys, they just couldn't get that and they still can't get the blues stuff right.

Payne continues his discussion of white musician's initiation into the blues tradition.

Payne: When Adelaide Hall--singer, I guess you heard of her years back. She had a blues piano player, no ragtime--jazz. They were at a place were all the musicians congregate you know after work, sitting there one trying to outplay the other. Art heard this piano player that Adelaide Hall had and he was tough, too. It just happened and Art asked him, "May I?" This guy just got through playing "Lighthouse Blues." Art got down there and started playing the same thing and outplayed him. He got up and said, "Nigger, where did you come from?" And he said, "Toledo." Mrs. Stewart, she heard about him and she was the one who had Adelaide Hall go over and hear Art play.[42] That's why they took him to New York that time. I didn't go with them but I knew he wasn't gonna make it, not with Adelaide Hall's band. You see she wanted a piano player. She didn't know what type of piano player Art was, but she always admired his work. You see he couldn't play behind a singer. She couldn't use him and I think she decided to not keep him.

Interviewer: Did he come back home?

---

[42] Art Tatum, file, Toledo Public Library, Letter to Felicity Howlett from Ella P. Stewart.

Payne: No. That's when he got started. He came back later, but he stayed around New York a little while.[43] One top announcer, when he heard Art Tatum, said he never heard so much piano playing. When we were down in front of the Cotton Club, Duke wanted Art to come and play and Art said, "I'm not ready for New York." "Just come on in play a number." When Art sat down and played the piano, Duke said, "You've been ready for New York a many years." New York just never knew about him.

Interviewer: Was he real happy about his success?

Payne: No, he never bragged about it. He didn't have to worry about that. He would see a piano, if it was too much out of tune he wouldn't play. No. He would go on a white job and the piano wasn't tuned he wasn't going to play it. You couldn't blame him because it was tough on his ear. That would be just like you hearing somebody trying to sing and hit a wrong note.

Interviewer: So he never talked about his success?

Payne: He didn't have to. He never was vain. He never bragged about nothing. He met his old friends down on Division Street.[44] Some of the people say, "What he want to hang down there

---

[43] Unknown news clipping. Chicago. 4 September 1941. Lists dates and locations of Tatum's annual concert tour. According to this article Tatum was often near Toledo.
[44] Stan Lee. "What Difference a Lifetime Makes," Toledo Blade 28 Feb. 1988: 1. Lee writes that the streets name meant exactly that. It once was a racial dividing line firm as the Berlin Wall, with blacks to the north and whites to the south.

for?" George White, he's a saxophone player, he and I worked together and they were asking us, "Well why do Art go down on Division Street and around?" I said, "That's where his friends are when he was here." And I said, "He never put his friends down." He never got too big for it. He would go down there with his old buddies and they liked to drink his beer and stuff; he never put them down. They were just like another buddy to him. You see a lot of them get there and you can't touch them. He didn't have to worry about it, because he knew they couldn't do nothing with his playing any how.

Interviewer: What after-hours places did you play in?

Payne: The Waiters and Bellmans. We played a lot of bigger clubs, also the Chateau La France and the golf club...

Interviewer: The Inverness Club?

Payne: Yeah, that was Chateau La France.[45] We played out

---

[45]Smith remembers that:

> he [Tatum] worked with me in my band for a long time. Some [of the clubs] were the Chateau La France and Tabernella Supper Club." Both were rum-runner hang outs and whites only restaurants according to James Lester (231)... "I expect I can say safely that we associated with one another and worked with one another off and on for about eight or nine years. He worked in my band just about the whole time I was working for the Chateau La France Club for Lou Breiner on Secor Road."

Smith continues,
> "Senior and I were partners and after Art went out of this area, we got a hold of Teddy Wilson."

there when Milton Senior had the band, but he had to have another piano player. He had to have two piano players because Art wouldn't take a contract. Mitch Woodbury wanted to know why. Art said, "I'll tell you." Remember the writer, there were big write-ups in the papers called or were these by Mitch Woodbury.[46] "He asked him why? Art said, "I'll tell you. If I feel like going to work, I'll go. I don't have no contract and if I don't show up, they can't fire me." He belonged to the musicians union but he wouldn't work under a contract for a long time. If he started enjoying himself in the afternoon somewhere and if he felt like he was going to have some fun he would turn down the work. That's the way I look at it. He didn't have to work. That's why I know Senior had two piano players because Dewey wasn't nowhere near the piano player Art was, but he was a good piano player for the style of band we had, but he wasn't no Art Tatum. We still had a piano player and had to have one out there if Art didn't show up and then again he may come in late. You never know. So now that's what you call power ain't it? The man paying you good wages. He never worried about no work. They were glad to get him.

They had a big name white band coming to one of the hotels downtown during the thirties--the rough times of the Great

---

[46] Payne is probably referring to Seymour Rothman.

Depression. They had Art Tatum doing the intermission, and he drew a bigger crowd than the band.

Interviewer: During the daytime what would Art be doing?

Payne: Oh he would probably be home sleep. If he wasn't sleeping he was on the piano and then again I don't know. I don't really know what recreation he did have. The only time I saw him was when we were together after we got through working nights.

Interviewer: Did Art go to Detroit and other places?

Payne: Yeah, he was up there. In fact, he could go anywhere; he didn't have to worry about nothing.

Interviewer: So he must have been content with being in Toledo?

Payne: He was. It wasn't like he could jump up and go where we wanted to. You see he had to depend on somebody. He went to Cleveland. I have taken him over a lot of times. He would go in a lot of night spots. Of course, he got paid for that. He would go around to different black clubs, of course whites weren't mixing then. He would go maybe just for an hour and all the black clubs around the neighborhood would be packed. When he left there, he would go to another one and the guy owning the place that he left would say, "Well, there goes the business for a while." The people would follow him to another club. He was out every night, I mean the weekends.

Interviewer: Who were some of the people with whom you and Art played?

Payne: Oh, there were quite a few around here; some were known piano players like Teddy Wilson who was here with Milton Senior. He [Teddy] was classed up there with Art at the time because he was Teddy Wilson, well he is still classed up there.

Interviewer: Was Art patient with other musicians?

Payne: Yeah, 'cause I know a lot of times when I first started working two jobs when he'd said, "Give me a ninth over here that sounds better." It was a full chord. I got so I used a lot of them, and he used a lot of ninths. He told you what to add. I would be playing the thing like it was written down. [For Art] I'd just add a note to it called a ninth or a diminished. So he kept bringing in more notes in case you don't know nothing, don't want to hear the wrong chord, you throw a diminished in there and nobody know whether you are right or wrong. You see a lot of ways... to get by. A lot of people would be playing and come up there in the bandstand, especially these white guys who'd ask, "What's the name of that?" or "How do you play that?" Well, when you are playing by ear you're up there playing these numbers what you call hidden numbers and been playing for a long time; you probably would forget some of them and ask Art what the name of it was. I couldn't tell the person; maybe I never rehearsed it. I know the number but never knew the name of it. You could hear it and go ahead and play it; you get your ear trained to it. One thing you could go in there and hit a bunch of keys, and Art would tell you what notes you hit, call them right off. That's what you call 'a real good ear.'

Interviewer: Did he get his piano training in Toledo?

Payne: Right at home. See, he was playing the piano when Slim Marshall [visiting in the Tatum home], a dancer working with me later on. [He said] Art sat down on his lap when he was four years old and he was picking out notes on the piano. He wasn't big enough and they would hold him in his lap and be playing tunes. He was just a natural and nobody can't say where it come from. He was just a genius. He didn't need no teacher. You see I wasn't there when he was coming up. When I first come to Toledo there was an island at Walbridge Park called Johnson's Island. A guy named Grubbs, he had a piano, and they brought it over on the weekends and Art and Freddie Taylor, the two of them. Freddie was on drums and Art playing piano out on that little old island. He was playing good piano then. So really I've never known him to take no lessons from nobody because I don't know who could teach him or show him anything. He could hear what you don't hear. I have asked him a lot of times the reason a lot of people can't catch your style, you have played the same thing over, when I first started working with him? I said, "Art, you changed different chords and things down there every time you go down again." He said, "Yeah, I believe in improving all the time." Now he would play that number down and when he go down again he is going to add something more to improve it. That's why they can't catch the style. He believes in improving and he used a lot of ninths. He had his finger here [traces between the thumb and index finger] split so he could hit the elevenths real fast.

Interviewer: Did Tatum have a surgeon do that?

Payne: Yeah, so it would be longer where he could reach, get almost a 13th out there, see. When you hit a ninth, you can hit an eleventh real fast. He just about had the whole thing where he could get. You see he couldn't just spread his little finger that far that's why he had them split. I don't know what else he had done to the other finger.[47]

Interviewer: Did he tell you why he did it?

Payne: Yeah. He said he could get the full scale. Some doctor did that for him. You see [I wasn't here when the surgery was done.]. I was in and out so much because that was the way black musicians had to work.

Interviewer: When he was telling you about it did it seem

---

[47] George Hoefer "The Hot Box" Notes to <u>Downbeat</u> 2 February 22, Personal papers of George Hoefer, Rutgers University Jazz Collection. Describes Tatum's hands but does not mention the surgery.

strange to you that he did it?

Payne: After he explained it to me [no,] because I know he was trying to hit a lot. It sounded like he wanted to have all the notes right in together so he could work real fast, but maybe he might skip just a fraction. But he would hear all them notes right together there. He could hit them so fast you couldn't tell the difference.

Interviewer: So he actually set about creating the style that he had?

Payne: It just come to him.

Interviewer: It came to him and he said, "I know what I want to do."?

Payne: He knew that. Just like a blind boy, you take a blind piano player, they create. I have heard guys jump up making like Jelly Roll Morton.

Payne explains one musician's imitation of Jelly Roll Morton's style.

Interviewer: Do you think Tatum's music was more jazz?

Payne: Tatum was jazz.

Interviewer: Tell me about the stride piano as part of the ragtime tradition.

Payne: Just strictly jazz--blues, ragtime. A lot of people think just because you are playing black music its jazz, but it isn't. Not all music is jazz; jazz is a different field.

Interviewer: You said there were a lot of musicians that came to Waiters and Bellmans. Do you remember any of them?

Payne: Yeah, quite a few of them. Benny James, the piano player who played for Cab Calloway. He was in Toledo. Art could out sell them anyhow. After Adelaide Hall's tough piano player heard him play he said, tickled me, he said, "Nigger, where did you come from?" He was playing so much piano. Art said, "Toledo," and he didn't want to believe it. He found out he was blind. Adelaide Hall come and heard him, and she booked him out.

Interviewer: I talked to the musicians union today and they said they don't have a record of Art Tatums ever belonging to Toledo's Musicians Union.

Payne: Yeah, he belonged to it, though.[48]

Interviewer: The Toledo one?

Payne: Yeah. I tell you why. You see, we had the black Local 286 and the white local was 15. Of course, way back then Norman Jones, my dad and uncle were the ones who started Local 286 here. They started Local 286, you see we had to get our own local. We were separate for a long time and a lot of the younger musicians

---

[48]Lester Smith personal interview. According to Smith:
  Although he [Tatum] played in several places at different times, he was one of the most popular fellows there was around here at that time, that is in music. He never did get with us in the Federation.

used to come by and say, "I think I'll join the white local." I'd say, "Go on down there and join them; you ain't getting no work." "No you jokers don't know nothing," I say, "Okay." I had a cousin in Chicago who was a musician. He said when we merged, you see we had to merge all over the country, Chicago, all of us. We were all under one head, you know and every one of my cousins and all them would work around music and in Chicago and New York. They said when they merged we're not getting the business, not getting any jobs. A lot of them have questioned me. I said when they call in they don't have no black secretary. They call in and want a black man. You know what they tell them? "Call back in about a half hour and see what we can do." And they say, "They are all busy."

They controlled it. People didn't want to believe me until some of the guys told me. I know that for myself on account that my cousins in Chicago said they lost jobs down there. Of course, now they are much different. There is no musician around here that can hold a decent job, like club work or so forth. [While Tatum was in Toledo] you had to pay the scale, the union scale. Sometimes they wanted to book you in the band for flat scale and say, "Who you got Duke Ellington or somebody?"

Interviewer: You were forced to take the job below scale anyway?

Payne: Yeah, so you might as well. Fats Mason[49] was a secretary for our local for many years and when they merged we had to merge with local 15; the white boys voted him in. Fats was our secretary, but the white boys liked him and he stayed until he died a couple years ago and they voted him in every year. They said he was the best secretary they ever had.

Interviewer: Did you ever hang out at the Frederick Douglas Center?

Payne: Yeah, years ago.

Interviewer: They said Tatum was there a lot, too.

Payne: We'd take rehearsing bands down there, too, in the afternoons. Some of the musicians weren't working in the daytime anyhow.

Interviewer: Did Art rehearse a lot with other people?

Payne: No he didn't. We never bothered about having him rehearse because you had to follow him anyhow.[50] By time he got through putting it down you might as well forget it.

Interviewer: Well, what was he doing at the Frederick Douglas Center?

Payne: Well, he'd probably go down there and if the piano

---

[49] Lester 48. Fats Mason was the drummer in the six-piece band that Tatum formed with Milton Senior in Toledo.
[50] Mayola Senior, personal interview, John Cleveland Collection.

was open he would be sitting down at the piano. Anywhere a piano was sitting, that's where he would be and wouldn't be in no hurry getting away. When the Douglas Center was on 10th Street there where the theater[51] is, they used to have different events on Sunday afternoons.[52] A lot of time he would play a few solos with other musicians and so forth. A lot of times the musicians come in just to play. Of course when Art come in you always let him be by himself because he was the star. Everybody liked him so well, he didn't have no enemies that I know of. He never was by himself. I've never seen him by himself. He always had his eyes with him, somebody to take him around. He had some cousins and so forth.

Interviewer: Did he walk with a cane or dog?

Payne: No.

Interviewer: Would Tatum call home or did he write home? Could he write in Braille?

Payne: I don't really know. You see I wasn't on the road with him. I never had no experience out of town with him, it was just all local.

Interviewer: Did he write music?

Payne: He might have written it in Braille. I've never seen any music he ever wrote; I can't say. I know he studied Braille, but whether he could write it, I don't know.

Interviewer: The contract that he made with Adelaide Hall he had an 'X' for his name.

Payne: I guess Stewart or somebody took care of him. Stewart booked him out and the thing of it is, you see, I didn't think they had the right people to handle artists like him because he was worth so much more money than what he was getting.[53] Anywhere he worked they got more money. Just like Liberace, of course he was a heck of a concert pianist, but he never had nothing on Art, no kind of way. All the musicians will tell you that. When the white boys tell you that you can believe it.

Interviewer: What kind of personality did Tatum have?

Payne: He never did argue at nobody that I heard of. In our clique we were all good friends so we never had that kind of thing. We might be ribbing somebody about playing something wrong and all that, "you ain't doing nothing," "that ain't nothing," "get up from there," things like that. We were ribbing each other.

He never did try to show anybody up or anything. He used to help somebody if they wanted it. If he wanted a chord, he'd say, "Well give me this, give me an augment or a diminished, it fits here

---

[53] See Contract to Stewarts, Telegrams, and Letters in the Toledo Public Library Local History Department file on Art Tatum. Payne is correct, the Stewarts acted as Tatum's agents.

better." That's all he would say, and you should know how to make those if you know your instrument. A lot of our boys go in there and they just got those three chords and they can't build up, amplify it because they don't know what they are doing.

Interviewer: I've heard people say he was an unusual person.

Payne: He was. He liked to help people out just like at those house parties. He didn't charge nobody, but he just done it to help somebody out. You know good and well if they couldn't pay their rent, cause I'm telling you Toledo was a rough place during the depression.

Interview of Mozart Perry and Clifford Murphy

Introduction

Mozart Perry also played piano in Toledo. He was younger then Tatum but he grew up in the same neighbor and cites Tatum as having influenced his playing. Mozart's brother, Rudolph Perry, was also a musician who remembered Tatum but he was ill when these interviews were being conducted and has since died.

This interview was conducted on March 31, 1992, at Murphy's, a jazz club in downtown Toledo. Also present was Clifford Murphy, the co-owner of Murphy's and a long-time bass player, who was born in Toledo. Although he was young when Tatum was in Toledo, Murphy also remembers the influence of Tatum on music and musicians in Toledo. Murphy remembered:

The only thing I can say really about Tatum, of course I'm a lot younger, I did go to school with his nephews and nieces, I lived four doors from him. I used to visit and go in the house, but I can't remember going in there too many times. There were times that he was there and I have heard him play the piano through the screen door but I couldn't get inside. When I was younger, you know, I don't know whether I was interested in music or fascinated by what I was hearing or what.[54]

Because Murphy is also a musician and Toledoan, his insights into the condition and history of the musicians are important to an understanding of Tatum's musical community. Murphy and Mozart are both recipients of Tatum's influence on the musical community in Toledo.

Mozart Perry still plays piano locally. His story includes Tatum and the musical community. Likewise, Perry's interview contributes to existing information on Tatum's musical impact on pianists in Toledo. Mozart agreed that Tatum's jazz teachers had only a minimal influence on his musical education and the popularity of jazz in Toledo. He also concurs that jazz can't be taught. Like

---

[54] Mozart Perry, personal interview, 31 March 1992.

Payne and Smith, Mozart believed that the musicians' union had some effect on Toledo's black musicians. Mozart and Payne concur that Tatum would help anyone.

Mozart recalls that all the musicians dressed in suits. He also remembers that Tatum and he both drank when they were teenagers. Although he stopped at 10 or 15 beers, Tatum did not.

Harry R. Reed, in his study, "The Black Tavern in the Making of A Jazz Musician: Bird, Mingus, and Stan Hope," writes that:

Young black musicians have always served a considerable period of their apprenticeship in black bars. There the young player learned acceptable professional standards. He worked to improve his technique, expand his repertory, extend the range of his instrument, and to internalize a positive attitude toward improvisation.[55]

Douglas Daniels also concludes that the socialization process of musicians taught them how to dress and as professional musicians how to handle the public--interviewers as well as fans.[56] Mozart's interview details this process.

---

[55] Harry Reed, "The Black Tavern in the Making of a Jazz Musician: Bird, Mingus, and Stan Hope," Perspectives of Black Popular Culture, ed. Harry Shaw (Ohio: Bowling Green Popular Press, 1990) 7.
[56] Douglas Daniels, "Oral History, Masks, Protocol in the Jazz Community," Oral History Review 15 (Spring 1987): 146.

Edited Taped Interview:

Mozart: I did take lessons at the Toledo Conservatory when I took lessons. I have been in Toledo ever since I was a little kid--three, four, five years old. I was born in Atlanta. We migrated here when I was about four or five years old.

Interviewer: So, was Tatum around then?

Mozart: Oh, yeah. Tatum is three years older than my brother. If he was living now Rudolph is 78. He was a trumpet player. He played with Tatum and they used to run together and drink together and been in my house. They stayed right around the corner from me, 4 or 5 block on City Park where Arlene, his sister, Tatum lives. Rudolph used to bring him by the house here when he was an early teenager. Rudolph was about 18 and Tatum was 21. You see, my brother is 78 and Tatum right now he would be about 81, if he was living.

Mozart and Murphy talk about Mozart's early start as a musician and the clubs that he played in. He remembers Tatum's influence on him in the following conversation.

Mozart: I didn't play with Tatum, but I used to sit and watch him because he played piano the same as I did only so much better.

Nobody played like Tatum. I got a lot of ideas from Tatum. You know, there will never be another Tatum. Oscar Peterson, if he was sitting here right now would tell you the same thing. I learned a lot, he showed me a lot and I'd play different songs.

There were a lot of clubs. The first club we used to hang out at was called Bellmans and Waiters Club. That was on Indiana. It's torn down now, years ago in the 500 block. That's before the M & L Club came around, maybe ten years later. That's when big names used to come here to Toledo, big named bands at Bellmans and Waiters on Indiana in the 500 block. Everybody from Ottawa Hills, from all over, white and black, used to come and hear the different bands play. We had a couple of big bands around here by the name of Jay Fred Terry and another big band from Toledo, Frank Lightfoot that had a 16 piece band. That was in the big band days.

Interviewer: Was the Waiters and Bellmans that big?

Mozart: Yeah, it was a pretty large club. It was along something like this but they had a big band stand didn't they?

Murphy: Yeah. They also had other sections where there could be an overflow for the crowd and another little section still could hear the band.

Mozart: They had a little dance floor in later years before Johnnie died, but starting out it wasn't a dance floor.

They continue their description of Waiters and Bellmans. Mozart also recalls that his brother, Rudolph, would bring many of the big name musicians and baseball celebrities such as Satchel Page to their family home at 626 Belmont. Alberta's Tea Room, another club in the 400 block of Belmont where white and blacks frequented, was also a favorite of Duke Ellington. Mozart also remembers Cab Calloway appearing at the Paramount.

Mozart: Tatum used to run around with all of the old time musicians because you could walk the street then and didn't have to look behind you. We could walk the street after we got off from work at two, three, four, and five o'clock in the morning. There were places to go, after-hour places. Nobody bothered nobody because everybody knew one another until after the Second World War and Korean War and everybody started coming over in this country then. Everybody in the city knew one another. When I was coming up as a kid if you did something wrong they would run you out of town, you wouldn't stay here. The neighbors used to watch one another houses, but now your neighbor will help rob you now, you don't know who your neighbors are. Nobody helps nobody. I remember you could leave your back door open. That's all over the country New York, California but not any more, little places the same, every place. I remember we used to leave our screen door unhooked and walk downtown as my mother and father did years ago, but those days are gone.

Interviewer: Would Tatum come back to Toledo a lot once he left with Adelaide Hall?

Mozart: Tatum used to come to Toledo every summer if he did leave. He would come back up on City Park and he had a chauffeur with him because he had very little vision in one eye and was going blind in the other one but he could see some. He used to shoot pool, take that bad eye and shoot pool and play cards and did everything. He was near-sighted more than completely blind like some people thought but he did go to blind school and took Braille music, he also could read other type of music, but didn't need it. He could hear anything he played. Tatum could play you but you couldn't play him. He could play anything and any style, but he had his own style. He was so fast he was just like lightning. His left hand was just as fast as his right. There will never be another Tatum. He wasn't handicapped. He used to play just like other kids did. He was just blind in one eye and had very little vision in the other.

You wouldn't have to treat him special. He used to try to do everything in the street, play football in the street. He did some of everything, shoot marbles. Tatum would run with everybody, run with some rough guys in town. I mean boxing, they didn't cut and shoot each other, you know, go to the bar and be drinking. It wasn't like it is now you know what I mean. Somebody get in an argument, don't four or five guys jump on you if you get in a fight, somebody would be fighting with fist and knock that guy down, next thing they would be at the bar best friends and end up buying drinks and forgot about it. But those days are gone. If you hit somebody now they will be looking for the gun and the next day do it.

Tatum never talked about nobody and was friendly with everybody. He was a good musician. The musicians in them days used to help one another instead of criticizing. He would go in, his ear was so good he would be outside. I remember I was playing at some little house-party playing piano. They used to have pianos all over town then. He would be walking down Erie street, all of those buildings torn down now. He would say don't play that young man, hold your hand like this and play it this way. He was always helping people. He never talked about nobody. He played with anybody whether they were bad or good, but nowadays these people don't help one another. He wanted music to be played right. I believe in playing music right, too.

Interviewer: When did Tatum start playing?

Mozart: His mother says he was a born genius. He started playing piano when he was five years old. He started playing by ear. The way he learned to play piano was these old self-player, you heard of the self-player that had rolls in it and he used to listen to rolls and look at the piano keys on the rolls when he was four and five years old and tried to play with the roll. His ear was so good that he just picked up off that and got his own style with the roll and played faster than the roll and played slow and played better than the guys on the self-player. He developed his own style from there.

Interviewer: Do you know of any teachers he had then?

Mozart: He had a teacher down in Cincinnati at the blind school. I saw a guy in Dayton one time, when I was working for the government, called Blind Clarence, a white guy. He said the teacher was so prejudice down there. This old Irish teacher he had; she was a classical piano player. Tatum would play classical like it is and then he would improvise it the way he wanted to play it and she would say "You ain't gonna never play, play it like this, play it like this. You ain't gonna never do nothing." Now she wasn't nothing but a teacher and that man went to Europe and went all over the country and nobody ever even heard of her. You know, I'm showing you how people were back in those days. "Play it like the music, you ain't playing that right." Even Blind Clarence told me that about the teacher. He was jealous of Tatum, that's what it was. He went to New York when he left Toledo. The first time he went to New York that was years ago. I remember when Tatum left here. I was a teenager. He went to New York and got his start in New York.

Played with a symphony band years ago and was director for one of those symphonies. They are critical. Patty Riskey said he heard Tatum. Patty Riskey played a concerto and Tatum sat right down and played it the way Patty Riskey played by listening at it and then he started adding his stuff to it and Patty Riskey said and this come over the radio back in them days, he said he never heard nobody like that in all his life--coming from Patty Riskey, critical like that where he criticized, you know he had to be good. He said there would never be another Tatum. He played before Duke and Eddie Haywood and all of us sitting at the table. Eddie Haywood, when he first heard Tatum had left Toledo, he said, "I ought to go back with a shovel and a pick, after I heard him I don't feel like playing no more." That's how good he was. That's something you know. The whole world thought of him as jazz. He could play classical. That man can play anything.

He played with everybody in the country. He played with every big band you could name. Everybody worthwhile playing back then he played with. Every old musician in the world knows about Tatum, from Paris to London and all through the United States.

Interviewer: Well, why do you think it took so long for Toledo to start recognizing Tatum?

Mozart: Why it took so long? Because the black people didn't back it until up to now. You see, we have to do something for ourselves. They had one man that came here and backed him, that was Billy Taylor, am I right? They should have backed Tatum a long time ago.

Interviewer: Tatum was on WSPD, wasn't he?

Mozart: Yeah. Tatum was on WSPD a lot of times.

Murphy: Also you had to remember, too, at one time even though there was jazz around this was a blues town. Even though the blues wasn't on the radio, I can remember going to all the clubs. They used to be packed playing the blues. Of course, there were a few clubs that had the blues and jazz. Other clubs, which back then it wasn't referred to as jazz, just music. I believe it was in my era when I started hearing the word jazz come up, the music we were playing was called jazz, I think it was because some people couldn't understand what was going on and to them it was just a whole bunch of things thrown into a kettle and therefore they called it 'jazz' which was something they couldn't understand.

Mozart: No, they couldn't understand.

Murphy: Even back in New York there were stories where white musicians used to go uptown and try to learn what these black musicians were doing. So to keep them from learning they would change the melody of a song. They would play something else that they know they couldn't hear.

Murphy: Even today they try to teach.

Mozart: They have to teach, but you can't teach it. It's something that's already in blacks.

Mozart and Murphy discussed the musicians union and its impact on Toledo musicians. They both recalled that Tatum was not a part of Toledo's musicians' union. Mozart continued with his perception of Tatum's personality.

Interviewer: Did you ever hear Tatum raise his voice about anything?

Mozart: No, I never heard him talk about nobody. He has never squawked on nobody about nothing. He was just a real person, nice person. He never got mad with nobody. I never seen him, he was just Art Tatum. Everybody respected him.

Interviewer: Did he ever get angry?

Mozart: No, never got angry.

Interviewer: How did Tatum dress?

Mozart: Everybody dressed back then. They didn't go like these guys now with their shirts out. Everybody had a suit of clothes just like you see him on this tuxedo. Everyday. When I was playing music, when I was working at home I was dressed like that everyday. That's what you call good musicians. They learn that from the older guys how to act. Stanley heard Art Tatum play when he was six years old, taking lessons. Probably he and my brother went to Stanley's house, Rudolph with Art Tatum. Art came to town, Rudolph was about 22 or 23 and Art was about 25 or 26. When they heard Stanley, maybe they were older than that. They may have been up in the late twenties, way back then, I don't remember exactly how old they were, but Stanley heard of Art Tatum he says, "Mama come back out of the kitchen and hear that man play the piano," Stanley's mother say they just dropped their plates right in the kitchen. "I never heard nothing like that in my life." She was in the kitchen working...[57]

Interviewer: Why do you think Tatum died so young?

Mozart: Forty-six years old. Well, Tatum--you know, you have heard of people having big mugs of beer, you have heard of the big glass where you drink out of the big mugs, you weren't born but you know. That's the time you could get beer for a nickel or dime, a big mug like that. A glass that big. A glass about that big and about that wide and he would drink that. We used to go down to a place called Chicken Charlie's on Lafayette Street, that's torn down, a big old gray building. Joe Western used to have that. They were half Italian and half black--looked like white guys. They were all right and had a place out there. When musicians come in town and Art Tatum would bet all of them that he would out drink them. He used to

[57] Stanley Cowell, personal interview, 25 May 1993.

drink 35 and 40 of those things. I was drinking then, I was a teenager and I drank about ten to twelve of them.

Conclusion

From the material gathered in Chapter IV, Tatum's public image does not deviate from that provided by his family and friends. His fellow musicians who are interviewed in this chapter contribute their perception of his skill and professionalism. They all agreed that the fun-loving Tatum, who played in the community, was a genius. The attributes ascribed to Tatum in this chapter include: generous, kind, patient, a perfect ear, and a willing teacher.

His skills as a pianist were unmatched by any jazz pianist. Payne suggests that he developed a style that could not be imitated, and Tatum created this style from his reach (which was expanded by an undocumented surgery), use of classics, and other familiar forms. Payne, like Herron, Butler and Casey (informants who were interviewed for Tatum's Community and Friends) remembered that he just liked to play. They remembered that he played for free to help at rent parties and other occasions while others, like Tandle, remembered that Tatum wanted fare remuneration for his skills outside of his community. His keen sense of business had been developed enough during these early days in Toledo to recognize his need to discern between bills of high and low denominations, according to Mayola Senior.

Tatum was the musician's musician. Perry said that "he could play classical, that man could play anything." He taught local musicians Payne, Smith, Perry, and Jackson some of his techniques. Tatum's success as a musician, no doubt, gained him popularity with the club owners. Payne recalls that the crowd would follow Tatum from one establishment to the other and when the crowd left, so would the business. Although he had this reputation, Perry remembers that he was never vain. However, Jackson considered Tatum's ego to be the source of competitiveness at cutting contests and his need to eliminate all other competitors. On several occasions, musicians referred to Tatum's loyalty. Although he did not have to be concerned about a job, he would not look out for himself only, but would see that other musicians had a job.

Tatum emerges from the interviews of the musicians as a young man who matures into a very competent professional musician. He was able to form his own bands, reject the pressures of the local musicians union and still work.

CHAPTER FIVE

Conclusions

Introduction

From the interviews in preceding chapters, a list of Tatum's character traits surfaced. These traits include: responsible, religious, dependent, independent, generous, considerate, accommodating, loving, family-oriented, obedient, committed, loyal, discreet, proud, and devoted. He was fun-loving (possessing a sense of humor), congenial, and mischievous. He was attracted by as well as attractive to women. He could be competitive, assertive, difficult, quick-tempered, and compulsive, but needful of comradery. He was also noted to be drug dependent. Tatum was considered a genius and a maverick.

Physical attributes that may have affected Tatum's genius were his tone acuteness, impaired vision, exceptional recall, and Braille-trained hands.

Among the people who influenced Tatum's character were: members of the black church, other musicians, neighbors, teachers,

227

family, and white friends/neighbors/colleagues. Performing in public establishments as well as private parties helped to shape his individuality. Political influences upon Tatum included racism, prohibition (alcohol availability), the musicians union, Ku Klux Klan, and the Mafia. His hobbies and his income were noted as significant to his development. Without an available piano, of course, Tatum would not have become the musician he was.

Influences of His Family

Tatum was the oldest of four children, with one brother dying at a very early age. Arlene recalls that the only other family member to live with them was their father's mother. Living with Art, Carl, and Arlene were their parents and paternal grandmother. Art began playing the piano at an early age without formal training. He pulled himself up onto the piano bench and started playing. With his mother's encouragement, he would play any song that he heard. His mother, however, decided that he should receive some formal training to "at least learn notes." This is apparently why he left for Cleveland at the age of 17 or 18.

His childhood seemed rather normal for a near blind child. Although we do not know for certain if he was born with cataracts or became blind from diphtheria and measles at three, Tatum did not let his blindness hinder his enjoyment of playing marbles or other childhood games. Tatum, together with his family's Sunday assistance, managed a large paper route. All attended church. His parents were pillars and founding members of their neighborhood church, Grace Presbyterian. His mother was a member of the missionary society at the time of her death. His father, an elder in the church, was its treasurer when it was established in the early twenties. Church attendance was part of the Tatum children's lives. Arlene remembers attending church all day on Sundays.

Tatum was loved by both his younger sister and brother. Arlene literally watched over her brother. When they were growing up together in Toledo, she would accompany him to places and activities which, at that time, were considered inappropriate for young girls, such as pool halls and shooting marbles. Arlene seemed very devoted to him, and Carl seemed to be proud to have him as a brother. It seems, however, that his mother's concern for Tatum's lifestyle was well founded. She and Carl acknowledged the difficult/free-wheeling lifestyle of musicians.

Likewise, Tatum was a devoted son and brother. Arlene's stories reveal Tatum's generous nature, recalling Tatum escorting their father, before his death in 1951, to sporting events across the country. It seems certain that Mildred Tatum's instructions on money left Tatum with the skills to manage his own. By every account, Tatum was seen as independent. His family's support made all the difference for Tatum.

Although Tatum learned the classics, he was not a classical pianist. He listened to the family radio and was influenced by the styles of Earl Hines and Fat Waller. As black music evolved, the blues--and later jazz in its most elementary state--came into being. These musical forms, which developed from the slaves' songs and spirituals, were referred to as "devil's music" by many class-conscious African Americans during this period. It is clear that the Tatum family did not share this view. Although they were a church family, Tatum's development of the stride and ragtime styles came from his exposure, in his home, to these forms of black music. If he had not had a family who supported this diversity, perhaps Tatum would have become a different pianist. Tatum lived in an atmosphere where his musical talents were not biased by prevailing attitudes. Instead, he was nourished and supported by a family that seemed to consider all music valid and honest. Seemingly, they did not exhibit the prejudices of other Negro congregates who considered any music outside of the spirituals and gospels to be a condemnation to hell. This was also a time in African American society when first generation families were struggling to maintain dominance over urban migrant families such as the Tatums. These struggles resulted in their offspring rebelling in ways that included the blues and jazz.

Assessment of the lives of Tatum's parents, confirms that they were strong people. In the midst of nearly overwhelming prejudice and racism, they like other black people of Toledo, found gainful employment, lived well, and grew prosperous. They succeeded in having their son, Carl, attain a college degree. This does not seem to be such an extraordinary task in today's world. However, the University of Toledo in 1927 had only 21 Negroes in attendance. Carl would, at that time, be one of the few blacks from Toledo's black community to break the educational barriers.

Carl's success, like Art Jr.'s, can in some ways be attributed to their strong family upbringing, with particular emphasis on the guidance and presence of a silent but strong father. When compared to Wheaton's analysis of Negro life during the period of Tatum's rearing, their family, as Arlene observed, was indeed one of the fortunate families in Toledo. Tatum Sr.'s life seems to be a testament to the early Toledo black father who raised his family, in spite of the odds. His presence must have profoundly affected Tatum Jr.

Arlene and Carl's accounts of their brother reveals the importance of family in the life of the great pianist. If he was unable to make it home, he would call for them to assist him, e.g., when he last appeared in Detroit, Arlene recalls Art calling home to tell her that he wasn't able to get to Toledo, but he wanted her to bring the family to Detroit's Keyboard Lounge.

Although Arlene and Carl's memories of Tatum have been previously published, their family life in Toledo has not been written about in any published account. Perhaps, more than any other work of its kind, this publication has helped us view Tatum in the context of his time and place in Toledo.

Of course, there are elements of Tatum's life, like any other celebrity, that remain obscure. One such instance, is the paternity of Orlando Tatum, Mia Tatum, and Arthur Tatum, Jr. Although Orlando Tatum is acknowledged by Arlene as Tatum's son, others have not been acknowledged by any family member. A New York Amsterdam article, found in the files of Tatum from the Rutgers University Jazz Studies department and written in 1965, contains a picture of Mia Tatum.[1] The caption reads "Art's Daughter" and said that Mia Tatum, "a pianist and vocalist, reflects many of the styling nuances of her late father (Art Tatum)." Many calls to the Amsterdam News and to various Tatums in the New York area revealed no additional information. Lester, in Too Marvelous for Words, confirms as false Tatum's paternity of both Mia and Arthur Jr. Likewise, Arlene has heard the rumors concerning Tatum's paternity of these children, but she has never seen them, nor have

---

[1] New York Amsterdam News: 6.

they ever come to meet the family. Tatum was sued for the care of Orlando upon his visit to Toledo in 1947. Arlene seems to have stayed in touch with Orlando and considers Orlando and Tatum to have had a close relationship. This closeness, however, was not confirmed in this research.

Interviews of Casey Jones and Harold Payne suggest that the Tatum household was open and friendly, not unlike other black homes at that time when life in the black community was different from what it is today. Jones remembers Tatum playing at the piano, and Payne remembers being one of the few people who was trusted by Tatum's mother to take care of him. Although Payne remembers a cousin having been involved in Tatum's care, Carl, according to Casey, seems to be the family member most frequently responsible for young Tatum. Newton's interview also reveals the close relationship that Tatum had with his mother and the family's propensity for fashionable attire. Although Lester's account suggests that both Mildred and Art Sr. misused alcohol, Arlene's recounting of her partying experiences, shows little evidence that alcohol was a problem for any family member, other than Art Jr.

Influences of Community and Friends

The history of Toledo is woven into the story of Arthur Tatum Jr. Many of the interviews highlight the later years of Tatum's residence in Toledo. Casey Jones, Jim Herman Butler, Gladys Herron, Mary Belle Shealy and Rose Newton have contributed essential insights into the literature on Tatum. Each of them was a leader in Toledo's black community and agreed that the black community during that period was not socially divided, as it is today. In other words, the geographical closeness of the community made most blacks socially accessible to each other, i.e., everybody knew everybody. Rose Newton said in her interview that stories of Tatum were passed on from her uncle, who would encounter Tatum in the local bars, to her mother, and to her. It does not seem a coincidence that all of those interviewed, with the exception of Shealy, were interviewed in the old Pinewood section of Toledo and still have affiliations with the area. Although it was not in this interviewer's knowledge, the Pinewood District seems to be the primary location of Toledo's long-established black families and is still home to Tatum's sister, Arlene.

The Pinewood District, referred to as the Bohemian Section by Lois Nelson, was also the district of poolrooms, recreational facilities, and local night spots frequented by Tatum. The dual identification of this district is significant from a cultural and historical perspective. Nelson, a white American, observes Tatum's community from an etic perspective, while those interviewed in this section, who are black, referred to this same community through an emic or insider's perspective. Consequently, the perspective of these interviews may be more valuable in that we view the history of black Toledo during the years 1909-1932 through the eyes of its participants. We understand from them what life was like for the first and second generation of blacks who came from the south to the northern ghetto life of Toledo. Their story is not the formulated theories of historians but tells the day-to-day experiences of a community that produced talents such as Art Tatum.

Although Casey Jones did not describe the social life of the Pinewood District's religious activities and night activities as either sacred or secular, he did indicate a dichotomy when he said, "It was something everybody seemed to do even if you went to church you didn't talk about where you went to the after-hours. It wasn't the conversation that you have been to an after-hours--you wouldn't brag about it." Jones's account also explains why many black people when queried about Toledo's gangsters and clubs have been reluctant to discuss them. Also, Jones alerts us to the need to examine the economics of Tatum's performances. Jones seems to suggest that the parties and after-hours engagements were a source of income for piano players, and Tatum, regardless of the social stigma connected to the music, performed at these. Shealy's interview confirms this. She made enough money playing piano during that period to significantly help herself and her mother. She, like Tatum, performed at the piano all night.

Herron and Butler also remembered Tatum's popularity at African American community functions. In fact, they recall that Tatum's music style eventually lured him away from the sacred music of his childhood. As Jim Butler and Gladys Herron recalled: "He didn't like to play too much church music though" and according to Gladys, "If he played church music he would jazz it up because that was his style of playing." If we compare their accounts with the others in Chapter III, we conclude that Tatum was not a recluse, that in fact, he was sociable typical of others his age. He played marbles as a child and had girlfriends. According to Butler, he was like the other guys. The community's closeness made this possible.

According to Shealy, Tatum played at Toledo's white establishments, recalling that he played at the Toledo Country Club. Shealy had some unpleasant experiences at some of the more elite white entertainment spots. She recalls not only the struggles of black male musicians but also those of the black female performers. She played at Toledo's popular Waiters and Bellmans Club, the local after-hours where Tatum honed his skills. Although many have argued that Tatum learned his style from classical musicians, Shealy adamantly denies this. She explains that Tatum never had a teacher, nor was he influenced by these classical teachers, adding that he could only have been self-taught. Other local musicians confirmed Shealy's observation.

Toledo's black community and Tatum could not escape the racism that was customary during this period but most of the interviewees did not disclose direct incidents. When Butler and Herron were asked about race relations in Toledo, they both remembered that the neighborhood streets had whites on one side and blacks on the other. Like Newton, who recalled the inception of the first black Catholic church, they also described instances in which the black community or individual was helped by whites. According to Butler there was no racial tension similar to today's. Butler said, "I still say that the white man doesn't hate black folks, he doesn't respect us."

Likewise, Butler suggests that Tatum's success was a result, in part, to his affiliation with Toledo mobsters of the twenties. Perhaps Tatum's affiliation and his talents insulated him from direct racial attacks. Ironically, even with the gang activity, life in the black community during Tatum's youth seemed less violent to Payne, Heron, and Butler, when compared to current media reports of violence and black-on-black crime, a concern of most Americans, including the people interviewed from Tatum's early years in Toledo. Each cited relationship among blacks as being the single most important element of change in Tatum's childhood community, when compared with the present.

Although Tatum must have been surrounded by violence and racism, he also would have found in the many community role models, the substance for building his self-esteem. Jones, Butler, and Herron allude to a self-contained black community where there were "black businesses on every corner and professionals who could be used as role models." Also, within Toledo's black community there was a concern for the other person and Tatum's childhood seemed to be built on a foundation of caring adults who were concerned about every child, not only his/her own. James Lester agrees that Tatum grew up among stable people and was part of a family and community with a settled lifestyle.

Tatum was found to be a likable person, although the people of Toledo related to him as another Toledo youth rather than as the legendary figure he later became. They suggest that certain qualities: his munificence and even temper, made him attractive to pal around with. These qualities, no doubt, added to his appeal as a pianist. His generosity and congeniality have been noted by other biographers. These were attributes that suggest that Tatum had assimilated into the role and lifestyle of the jazz musician. Such are adjectives and descriptions used in reference to Tatum's personality: jovial, Mama's boy, family man, loving, protective, uncle-like, admirable, congenial, not temperamental like other artists, same all the time, never saw him mad, plenty of girlfriends, and generous. Newton said that Tatum's family "dressed." Later, Tatum kept his "Mama" in style. Whatever money he made, he sent it home. His sister used to wear large diamonds and other expensive things."

Newton's observation on Tatum's sense of style and fashion seems accurate. Years after he left Toledo, Billie Holiday called him "The Banker," because he always wore a three-piece suit and was, as Sylvia Syms said, "A very dignified gent." If examined closely, photographs reveal nicely tailored suits.

From his days in Toledo until his death, Tatum seemed to be characterized as a generous and likable person. Lester concludes that Tatum's need for comradery and his piano playing went hand-in-hand. According to previous interviews, he was wherever a party was occurring and he seemed to enjoy playing. Lester agrees that certainly as a teenager he provided music for many social occasions. A cousin and Herron remembered that everyone wanted Art to play the piano so they could sing and dance. Although the Toledo establishments he played in may have not been as glamorous or well known as those in California and New York, he had many opportunities to play: house parties, after-hours, a few black clubs, and white speakeasies, some owned and operated by white mobsters.

Other people in Tatum's Toledo community, although not included in this volume, have suggested that Tatum was a likable and popular person. Despite his disability, people like to be around Tatum. A former English/American History teacher of Tatum's, Mrs. Morrison, recalled during the years 1922-24 that he was mischievous, sweet natured, and well liked. Tatum's personality seems to run the gamut; however, everyone agrees that he was usually likable. Felicity Howlett told me at the Tatum Celebration that I would be surprised by what others said about Tatum, stating that no one ever had a bad thing to say about him.

Many biographers have referred to the limited role of women in Tatum's life. However, beginning with Gladys Herron and in his early years in Toledo, Tatum enjoyed the companionship of women. This is not to say that he was a womanizer or chased after women, there are no sources to document this, but he did have girlfriends. According to Herron, he had "girlfriends." Neeland also said that on her visits to his house, she frequently saw him with a woman. Others have referred to Tatum's relationships, including Eddie Barefield, a musician who lived near Tatum in the early 1930s. Sylvia Sims remembered Tatum affectionately. Lester agrees with other biographers that Tatum had limited encounters with women but refers to the birth of his son, Orlando, by Marnette Jackson, in 1933.

Rudolph Perry, who knew Tatum in Toledo, was asked by Lester how Marnette and Tatum met. Perry said that "just from going around places. They got together like young people do, you know. They used to go on rides around together, Art brought a car, we used to ride around with him--1931 Ford. Used to take her on the boat, moonlight [probably the same boat rides Grace Herron refers to]." Perry goes on to say that "he didn't run too much with girls--not too much," seeming to suggest that Tatum did have girlfriends. It appears as if Tatum's relationships with women were typical. Tatum, generally, conducted his life in a private and conservative manner. In fact, Tatum seemed to be conservative in every area of his life except substance abuse.

These interviews contribute more information about Tatum's personal life in Toledo. They contradict much of his later public image concerning his relationship with women, his personality, and generosity. The Tatum image has been left intact by those interviewed. For lack of any other information, it seems valid to conclude that Tatum was generally well liked. Many have said that there is more to the story of Tatum than frequently reported; this biographer did not find any information to support this in Toledo. However, if we read the interviews, we can certainly get the flavor of Tatum's community and what it must have been like for him growing up in Toledo. This research, also, describes how racism gave him a forum in which to mature and experiment as a pianist, to the end of refining his style.

Influences of Toledo's Musical Community

When we review the data on Tatum offered by Toledo musicians, we get a clearer picture of him as a young musician. Harold Payne contributes anecdotes that confirm Tatum's unique personality, his ability to overcome his handicap, and his great talent as a musician. Tatum's early life in Toledo as a musician in various bands have already been highlighted by interviewers such as Mayola Senior. Others give us the picture of Tatum as a considerate and talented band member. Jack Jackson and Mozart Perry remind us of what it was like to experience the great Tatum's presence at an early age.

As biographer Lester has noted, Tatum learned from piano rolls and the radio. Payne, in his interview, refers to his musical abilities as a gift. However, upon examination of this study's interview information and research from other Tatum scholars, the data suggest that the young Tatum with limited vision worked hard to develop his talent, listening to the piano player at church, absorbing the musical influences of his home. He honed his skills as a child by listening to other musicians; later, when his mother recognized his talent and sent him to piano teachers, he mastered the lessons. As a young musician, he built on his experiences with other musicians to create a style and technique that made him famous.

It has been cited that Tatum played the piano for several reasons. The piano's capacity to be played independently of other instruments is one asset for jazz musicians, allowing them freedom to study, experiment, and perform alone. This was probably more true for the visually impaired Tatum. A piano and a guitar, possibly, were available in the Tatum home, but music, in some form, certainly became an inescapable choice for the young musician. Because of his visual impairment, he would have experienced a certain amount of confinement, making the piano a more attractive instrument for him. Therefore, it would seem that Tatum became a master of his environment, in part, through his playing.

The musicians in this research remind us that there were other piano players performing during Tatum's years in Toledo. Perry and others had to compete with Tatum's popularity. Jackson even recalls that Teddy Wilson, who was in Toledo at the time, was jealous of him. Although there was no one who could outplay Tatum, he could not perform at all of the available jobs for pianists.

Sometimes, the determination of who would get what job was based on who could read music and play with groups in white clubs. At other times, when the union came into existence as Payne reminded us, the decision of who was hired depended on who was the secretary of the musicians' union. In Toledo when Tatum played, there were separate unions for black and white musicians. Many have said that Tatum did not belong to the union; there are no records of his union membership.

According to Payne, Tatum's membership in a union was unimportant because Tatum made his own rules and caused others to accommodate him. Either they played with two piano players, Tatum and his substitute; or the other musicians had to pick him up, because in most cases their employment depended on him. Tatum seemed also to have set the trend for upcoming musicians. Teeny Brown remembers that as a teenager Tatum was the only person for whom the piano was unlocked at the Frederick Douglas Center.

Tatum also pioneered for black Toledoans, performing on the radio and in many night spots from which they had previously been barred. Many of the people interviewed in this study reminded us of the role that musicians have played in this country's struggle with the on-going problems of racism. As Tatum did, musicians have been able to break through the cultural barriers between white and black communities and have also been the transmitters of black culture, to the rest of America. African Americans, although denied access to other arenas, have been welcomed as entertainers. However, it is not often that we hear statements such as the one made by Payne, about Tatum telling the owner of the club that he would not play if other blacks were not permitted into the club. This loyalty was another characteristic of Tatum's that endeared him to other musicians.

Many musicians have said that Tatum was always helpful. He did not put other people down, and he chose to associate with his same friends when he came to visit in Toledo. His success was never a source of arrogance. He remained likable and independent throughout his life. It was as if Tatum understood the dynamics of people. Many scholars have said that Tatum's love of people demanded that he play the piano, creating for him an endless supply of friends. He seemed very loyal to his fellow musicians. David G. Hyltone, like Harold Payne, recalled that Tatum accepted the job at WSPD only after his friend had been given a job also. According to Eddie Barefield, the job at WSPD allowed Tatum to purchase his first car, a Model A Ford, which his cousin, Chauncey Long, or friend would drive for Tatum and which eventually Tatum drove up a tree.

Typically, Tatum's drinking did not jeopardize his job. In fact, Tatum was known equally as well for his capacity to consume beer as he was for his piano playing. If the letter from Bert Hall is read carefully, we can infer that Tatum's drinking caused him to be late for performances. His drinking is frequently mentioned in other works on Tatum, but rarely does any writer list alcohol as a dominant characteristic of his personality. Smith said about Tatum's drinking that "his favorite drink was beer... he could sit and drink a case of beer." Many have alluded to alcohol as a contributing factor in his death, but Payne only acknowledges Tatum's need to have fun. Musicians who played with Tatum in Toledo had very fond memories of Tatum and considered him a friend.

Tatum's ability as a teacher after he left Toledo is frequently documented by other biographers. In Mozart Perry's interview we see the same Tatum--someone willing to help. Perry said that he studied Tatum and learned from him. Perry would visit the Tatum household to play on their piano. He also remembers that the piano was a popular instrument in their neighborhood. Others who hung out in Toledo during this time also remember Tatum's kindness as a teacher. Jackson, another musician who learned from Tatum, remembers his style as unorthodox. Jackson also recalls that Tatum's ego was responsible for his appearance at many of the cutting contests, such as the one with Bud Powell.

Although Mary Belle Shealy only met Tatum once, she had friends in common with him. As you read her interview, many of the prevailing attitudes of the times can be detected, e.g., she was taught the classics, considered to be the only good music. She defines jazz as "something you can dance to." Similarly, Perry defines jazz as "some of this and some of that." Jackson, in his interview with John Cleveland, said that "when that type of music came in it was, to me, kind of unorthodox." It becomes obvious that they are struggling with the same phenomenon that others have struggled with, that is, what is the origin of jazz and how is it defined? Jazz was not as popular in Toledo as the blues. Murphy, Mozart, and Payne remembered that many people didn't understand jazz. Also, according to Shealy there were not any teachers at that time in Toledo who could have taught Tatum his style of playing. Although not a jazz pianist, Shealy suggests that a good, pleasant personality would have earned Tatum quite a good income.

Tatum was not alone in being a self-taught jazz pianist. Some of the Tatum's contemporaries were also self-taught: Eubie Blake, Scott Joplin, and Thelonius Monk. His style was greatly influenced by James P. Johnson who privately tutored Thomas "Fats" Waller (1904-1943). Johnson, however, "received private lessons as a boy and unlike his predecessors had a good knowledge of the European classics. Art Tatum help to perfect his trio combination of piano, bass, and guitar. Tatum's beginnings with his own band were in Toledo where, during Prohibition, he started a six-piece band that included Milton Senior.

Tatum also pioneered the art of soloing piano to which he remained true, even after its popularity waned. Although ragtime was the earliest documented form of jazz, Tatum perfected the stride piano and what is called 'soloing.' When we look at the history of jazz performance and black performance in general, it is no surprise that Tatum perfected the art of soloing. Not only was he technically able to play all the parts, but economically it had its advantages. Cutting sessions demanded more from the musicians as they competed against each other. Black vaudeville and minstrelsy created an image or expectancy of African American entertainers and entertainment by white audiences that in many cases affected performance. According to Douglas Daniels, many jazz musicians become socialized into a protocol that allowed for these variations. If we study Tatum's performances in public places as opposed to after-hours and rent parties and his response to their respective audiences, we can conclude that Tatum's style was also a response to the era in which he played and to his private vision.

The jazz community also offered Tatum an alternative community in which his disability was not considered a handicap. Tatum dominated the jazz community where he spent a good deal of his time. Perhaps it compensated for his lack of vision and other shortcomings that he might have experienced. This may explain the marathon sessions at the piano and his being within the jazz community instead of home. Although his home was loving, the jazz community provided a warm atmosphere which was not available anywhere else in white America for a vision-impaired black male. The jazz community allowed for black male frailty and transferred the black male's potency to the music. Within the jazz community Tatum defined his boundaries physically and musically. He often would arrive early to a club date to arrange the seating and gain familiarity with the surroundings.

While extracting information about Tatum's character traits the following inconsistencies emerged. Although we are not sure what were the causes of Tatum's drinking, many speculations may be made which may be the thesis of additional research. Some of which could be his fear of further blindness or childhood neglect. Arlene's interview, however, does not give us these answers. While Lester suggests that his parents drank, there are no other sources that verify this. Arlene, in her interview, refers to Tatum drinking large quantities of milk, suggesting that he had early symptoms of stomach problems. While these are both compulsive and obsessive patterns of behavior, usually associated with genius traits, this could also be a response to his environment rather than his internal make-up.

Another inconsistency that emerged was his love of family,

while not pursuing a relationship with his son, Orlando. Although Arlene suggested that they were very close, Lester argues that there was no relationship established between the two. Speculative results in this research may not be disregarded because Arlene's insights help to define Tatum's family environment and also help us to determine his innate abilities. If her story is distorted, many of the details of his early life may be hidden.

Another pattern also emerged regarding Tatum's character traits. Everyone seemed to suggest that he was pleasant, generous and kind. Neither Lester nor Howlett found anyone who disliked Tatum. It seems impossible for everyone to agree that he had no personality flaws. Did he work at being liked to combat his loneliness? If this is the case, this may reflect the effects of an environment that rejects handicapped people. If Tatum did not work at being liked, then these characteristics were part of his internal make-up. However, a mystery attributed to Tatum's love of privacy leads us to speculate on the value of these observances.

REFERENCES & RESOURCES

- Allen, Barbara. From Memory to History: Using Oral Sources in Local Historical Research. Nashville: American Association of State and Local History, 1981.

- Anonymous article. Toledo Blade 1 May 1923.

- Anonymous article. Toledo Blade 3 July 1922.

- Anonymous article. Toledo Blade 5 May 1923.

- Anonymous article. "Leafings." Toledo Topics March 1928: 10.

- Anonymous article. "Plantation Drinking Song." Toledo Topics. March 1929: 22.

- Anonymous article. "What to See Where To Go." Toledo Topics Dec. 1927-Nov. 1929: 1-3.

- Anonymous article. "Unlock the Piano." Toledo Blade 27 January 1992 Peach Sec.: 1.

- Art Tatum: The Art of Jazz Piano. Videocasette. Produced and directed by Howard Johnson. Channel 4. WXTV, 1988.

- "Art Tatum Sued for Son's Care." Toledo Times 25 June 1947: unknown

- Asante, Moledi. The Afrocentric Idea (Philadelphia: Temple U. Press) 141).

- Batz, Bob. "Stop All that Jazz? Never, Says 'Mo' Perry." Daily News Entertainment: 7.

- Bennett, Leronne. Before the Mayflower. Baltimore: Penguin Books, 1961.

- Bushnell, Garvin. Jazz from the Beginning. Ann Arbor: University of Michigan Press, 1990.

- Butler, Jim and Gladys Herron. Personal interview. 12 June 1992.

- Cody, Watson C. "New York Theater." Toledo Topics. November 1927: 21.

- Campbell, Joseph. The Power of Myth. New York:

Doubleday, 1988.

- Celebrating Tatum. By imelda hunt. Murphy's Jazz Club. 20 February 1992.

- Charles, Russ. Personal interview, 11 October 1993.

- Cole, Edrene. "Blacks in Toledo: A Resource Unit for Elementary Teachers." Thes. U of Toledo, 1967.

- Cone, James. The Spirituals and the Blues. New York: Seabury Press, 1972.

- Conover, Willis. "An Interview with Art Tatum." Keyboard. October 1981: 28+.

- Cowell, Stanley. Telephone interview. 25 May 1993.

- Daniels, Douglas H. "Oral History, Masks, and Protocol in the Jazz Community." Oral History Review 15 (1987): 143-164.

- Doerschuck, Bob. "An Art Tatum Biography." Keyboard Magazine. unknown:22.

- Duckett, Alfred. "What a Blind Man Sees," New York Age Defender 29 May 1954: Cl.

- Dunaway, David K. and Willa Baum. Oral History: An Interdisciplinary Anthology. Nashville: American Association of State and Local History, 1984.

- ---, How Can I Keep From Singing: Pete Seeger. New York: McGraw-Hill Book Company, 1981.

- Elder, R. Interview. 12 May 1993.

- Feagin, Joe. Racial and Ethnic Relations. New Jersey: Prentice Hall, 1989.

- Feather, Leonard. "The Rhythm Section." Esquire. October 1944: 4.

- Friends of the Toledo Public Library. 1993 Historic Calender.

- Guralnick, Peter. Searching for Robert Johnson. New York: E. P. Dutton, 1989.

- Hareven, Tamara. "The Search for Generational Memory." Oral History: An Interdisciplinary Anthology. Ed. Willa Baum and David K. Dunaway. Nashville: American Association of State and Local History, 1984. 248-263.

- Hazzard-Gordon, Katrina. Jookin. Philadelphia: Temple University Press, 1990.

- Hoefer, George. "The Hot Box." Notes to Downbeat. 2 February 1932. Personal papers of George Hoefer. Rutgers University Jazz Collection.

- Howard, Joseph A. "The Improvisational Techniques of Art Tatum." Diss. Case Western Reserve, 1980.

- Howlett, Felicity Ann. "An Introduction to Art Tatum's Performance Approaches: Composition, Improvisation, and Melodic Variation." Cornell University, 1983.

- Illman, Harry R. Unholy Toledo. San Francisco: Polemic Press Publications, 1985.

- Jackson, Jack. Interview with John Cleveland. 5 April 1982.

- Jeffers, Dereck and Moira Lerner. Harrison's Principles of Internal Medicine.

- Jepsen, Jorgen Grunnet. Discography of Art Tatum and Bud Powell, 1961.

- Johnson, Everette. "A Survey of the Negro Families in the Pinewood Avenue District of Toledo, Ohio." 1923.

- Jones, Casey. Personal interview. 17 April 1992.

- Laubich, Arnold and Ray Spencer. Art Tatum: A Guide to his Recorded Music. Scarecrow Press: N.J., 1982.

- Lee, Stan. "What Difference a Lifetime Makes." Toledo Blade 28 February 1988: 1.

- Lester, James. Too Marvelous for Words. New York: University of Oxford Press, 1994.

- Levine, Lawrence W. Black Culture and Black Consciousness. Oxford University Press: London, 1977.

- Locke, Alain. Sounds of Blackness, From Africa to America, 1994 pg. 46

- Lyons, Lens. The Great Jazz Giants. New York: DeCapo Press, 1983.

- Moreland, Geraldine. Interview. Afro-American

Experience in Toledo 18 April 1978. Toledo Public Library.

- Neeland, Fredricka Scott. Personal interview. 25 May 1993.
- Nelson, Lois. Personal interview. 24 March 1992.
- Newton, Rose. Personal interview. 12 June 1992.
- Null, Gary. Blacks in Hollywood: The Black Performer in Motion Pictures. New Jersey: Citadel Press, 1975.
- Ogen, Kathy J. The Jazz Revolution: Twenties America and the Meaning of Jazz. New York: Oxford University Press, 1989.
- Okihiro, Gary. "Oral History and the Writing of Ethnic History." Oral History: An Interdisciplinary Anthology. Ed. Willa Baum and David K. Dunaway. Nashville: American Association of State and Local History, 1984. 195-211.
- Payne, Harold. Personal interview. 20 March 1992.
- Perry, Mozart and Murphy, Clifford. Personal interview. 31 March 1992.
- Porter, Tana Mosier. Toledo Profile: A Sesquicentennial History. Toledo: Toledo Public Library, 1987.
- Reed, Harry A. "The Black Tavern in the Making of A Jazz Musician: Bird Mingus, and Stan Hope." Perspectives of Black Popular Culture. Ed. Harry B. Shaw. Bowling Green: Bowling Green University Popular Press, 1990. 7-21.

- Roger, Ray. Personal interview. 16 April 1992.
- Rothman, Seymour. "Art Tatum's Toledo Years." Toledo Blade 30 June 1985, mag. sec.: 12.
- ---. "The Art of Tatum." Toledo Blade 14 June 1970: 6.
- Russ, Charles. Personal interview. 11 October 1993.
- Russell, Joan. Personal interview. 15 March 1992.
- Russo, David. Families and Communities: A New View of American History. Nashville: American Association For State and Local History, 1974.
- Russo, Mary. Personal interview. 20 February 1992.
- Scott, John. Personal interview. 15 September 1993.
- Senior, Mayola. Interview with John Cleveland. 11 November 1981.
- Shadie, Beverly. "Purple Gang." Montage November 1993: 8.
- Shaw, Harry B. Introduction. Perspectives of Black Popular Culture. Ed. Harry B. Shaw. Bowling Green: Bowling Green University Popular Press, 1990. 1-6.
- Shealy, Mary Belle. Personal interview. 20 March 1992.

- Smith, Clarence G. Interview. Afro-American Experience in Toledo. 18 April 1978. Toledo Public Library.
- Smith, Mr. and Mrs. Lester. Interview with John Cleveland.

21 November 1981.

- Spellman, A.B. Giants of Jazz. Virginia: Time Life Records, 1982.

- Starr, Louis. "Oral History." Oral History. (American Association for State and Local History: Tennessee, 1984) 5.

- Stewart, Ella P. Interview. Afro-American Experience in Toledo. 18 April 1987. Toledo Public Library.

- Stocking, Kathleen. Letters from the Leelanau: Essay of People and Place. Ann Arbor: The University of Michigan Press, 1990.

- Southern, Eileen. The Music of Black Americans. New York: W.W. Norton, 1983.

- Tatum, Art. Improvisation, No. 2: Piano Interpretations of American's Outstanding Songs by Art Tatum. Robbins Music Co., 1946.

- The Tatum Legacy. Videocassette. Developed by John Cleveland. prod. Toledo Public Library and WGTE-TV, 1983. 27 min.

- Taylor, Arlene. Interview with John Cleveland. 6 November 1981.

- ---. Telephone interview. 9 September 1993.

- ---. Personal interview. 17 April 1992.

- Thompson, Paul. The Voice of the Past. New York: Oxford

University Press, 1988.

- Vallongo, Sally. The Genius of Jazz: Toledo Celebrates Tatum, January 15-February 16, 1992. Program.

- Wheaton, E.L. "The Social Status of the Negro in Toledo, Ohio." Thesis Bowling Green State University, 1927.

- Williams, Francis. Interview. Conversation Phil Schaap. WKCR, unknown. 3 November.

- Williams, LeRoy T. "Black Toledo: Afro-Americans in Toledo, Ohio, 1890-1930." Diss. University of Toledo, 1977.

- Williams, Martin. The Jazz Tradition. New York: Oxford Press, 1983.

- Woodbury, Mitch. "Mitch Woodbury Reports." Toledo Blade 13 February 1947: unknown.

- Work, Monroe. Negro Year Book, 1925-1926. Alabama: Negro Yearbook Publishing Co., 1926.

Made in the USA
Lexington, KY
30 September 2018